THE
WAR
FOR
FUNDRAISING
TALENT

THE
WAR
FOR
FUNDRAISING
TALENT

AND HOW SMALL SHOPS CAN WIN

JASON LEWIS

gatekeeper press
Columbus, Ohio

Published by Gatekeeper Press
3971 Hoover Rd. Suite 77
Columbus, OH 43123-2839
www.GatekeeperPress.com

ISBN: 9781642370003
eISBN: 9781619848702

Printed in the United States of America

To Ronnie Collins,

who gave me the opportunity
to discover fundraising as meaningful work

Table of Contents

Introduction 1

The War for Fundraising Talent 9

Hounded by Charities 27

Owning Our Fears 41

Moving On 55

Harvard's Fundraiser 59

A Tale of Two Ryans 77

A New Definition of Fundraising Talent 95

Conclusion... 115

Recommended Reading............................. 119

Fundraising Planning Models 123

Introduction

I THOUGHT I HAD IT ALL figured out. I was having a great deal of success as a major gifts officer at a large health charity in Washington, DC. This role was unlike my previous roles in small shops, where my performance was contingent on an ineffective schedule of events and appeals. My new boss, Danielle, had a good deal of confidence in me; I was quickly given the opportunity to expand my breadth of experience as a fundraising professional.

It was an exciting and invigorating time in my career. My job description was not unlike most major gift roles; almost like clockwork, we traveled the country asking high-net-worth individuals for multi-year pledges. Danielle wanted to learn as much as I did and she was eager to work as a team. She thought outside the box and allowed me to grow in my skills as a fundraiser. We raised a lot of money for a cause we were both very passionate about.

While working long hours and doing lots of traveling, I was also beginning grad school. My concern for the challenges small shops experience was growing, and I was grateful the program allowed me to focus my research on improving fundraising outcomes for smaller nonprofit organizations. The combination of my work experience and my academic research began to shape my understanding of how effective fundraising really works.

Despite my relative youth and inexperience, I began to get an itch to begin consulting. My ambition drove me to accept a job offer negotiated over the phone with a company I'd never heard of, working for a man I'd never met in person, headquartered in Reno, of all places. What was I thinking? I abandoned a role where I was finding great success for a consulting role for which, in many ways, I was unprepared. I'd spent the previous ten years admiring the ease with which some of my mentors had successfully transitioned into consulting. I was eager to follow the same path.

While the Reno shop described itself as a full-service agency, they weren't offering much more than grant writing services to small, faith-based organizations. My experience in similar nonprofits made it easy for me to relate to these organizational leaders and my recent track record of successfully asking for big gifts was attractive to them. I presented fundraising seminars to audiences in hotel conference rooms up and down the eastern half of the United States. I met passionate leaders of organizations who were doing good work against unbelievable odds. They seemed to fear fundraising more than anything else, and they hoped my seminar would help them unlock the secret they might have overlooked. Deep down, they wanted to hear that effective fundraising could come without a lot of hard work, persistence, audacity, and thick skin.

Most of the organizations didn't buy what I was selling, not because they weren't convinced, but because they were broke. As is generally the case, grant funding was limited, and very few of the applications would be funded. Overpromising and under-providing was our modus operandi. Mike wanted me to sell high-margin contracts extremely short of the actual deliverables. He was selling a quick fix; I wanted our clients to grasp a fundamental solution. Mike's goals and mine were incompatible, but I was too naïve to understand this—and he was too corrupt to tell me.

In early 2007, Faith-Based Solutions received a $500,000 federal grant from the Faith-Based & Community Initiative to teach nonprofit organizations how to apply for federal government grants. Part of the grant terms required $200,000 of the funds to be distributed to sub-grantees. These grants were never paid.[1]

Anyone who remembers 2007 knows the economy was beginning to collapse. Our family was leasing a townhome in one of the most expensive parts of the country, and my wife Erika was pregnant with our fourth child. I wanted to be on the fast track to consulting and genuinely believed the wisdom I'd gathered thus far was sufficient. I was wrong. Not only had I put my career in jeopardy, I had put my role as provider to my growing family in jeopardy as well. These were some of the most challenging and refining months of my life. I eventually landed another job and found a great place to start over; as most fundraising professionals are aware, we can recover quickly.

In 2015, Mike was sentenced to 2½ years in federal prison, three years of supervised release, and 100 hours of community service. Plus, he was ordered to pay $200,000 in restitution to the U.S. Department of Health and Human Services and $100,899 to the IRS for his convictions on theft of federal grant money; and failure to pay employment taxes.[2]

During those six months, I interacted with many people and observed a lot of organizational behavior. Every conversation in every seminar echoed a similar theme: small shops rely heavily on some of the most ineffective methods of raising support. They were determined to change the world, yet so fearful of fundraising that they could hardly call it by its name.

I observed highly optimistic leaders who were strong believers in people and purpose, but who routinely hired the

---

1   www.justice.gov/usao-nv/pr/man-who-operated-reno-consulting-firm-sentenced-2-12-years-prison-theft-and-failing-pay. Accessed November 8, 2017.

2   Ibid.

wrong people for the wrong reasons. If, on the rare occasion such an organization could hire an individual with the potential to be a high-capacity fundraiser, the organization lacked the culture to keep her longer than eighteen months. These rising stars left in search of adequate support, constructive feedback, and the necessary supervision even the best of us require.

Most of the nonprofit sector is entrenched in new donor acquisition. A constant focus on acquiring new sources of funds is not sustainable fundraising. In fact, it's not a sustainable business model for any industry. Services such as the ones we were selling in Reno were a quick fix fueling an addiction. I realized if I were going to make a difference, I'd have to swim upstream.

It's been ten years since Reno. Now I'm doing consulting in a much better place. Because of Reno, I resolved to learn more about myself and other people. Much of this book is designed to encourage fundraising professionals—and those who hire them—to better understand themselves and the organizational culture where they operate.

An Honest Yet Hopeful Critique

Today's retiring generation of fundraisers has admirably stumbled its way through a profession reliant on other domains, followed by an incoming generation questioning whether what they're inheriting is best practice—or simply what made the most sense at the time. Adding to this tension is our awareness that technology will insist on its own way, and our hesitancy to adapt to give it a proper place.

Today's donor is looking for new terms of engagement to ensure that they too are given a meaningful place at the table. As we begin this period of transition, the sector has expanded on a global scale, and talented fundraising professionals are in high demand around the world. These high performers are generally working for the largest organizations that, we presume, have not only larger and more affluent constituencies, but other advantages we can only envy.

After years of observing the practices of professional fundraising, this book is my first attempt at putting two decades of meaningful work on paper. To ensure my message doesn't get lost in the crowd—and in keeping with my contrarian nature— I've chosen several unique lenses through which to view our challenges and opportunities.

We'll gain perspective on what's really happening with the help of those who sought to better understand addiction. We'll consider a different take on recent events in the United Kingdom that have brought our profession under fire. And we'll look at the experiences of several fundraisers: one of Harvard's greatest, two young men who've made remarkable strides very early in their fundraising careers, and my own.

This book is an honest yet hopeful critique of professional fundraising, intended especially for small shops that find it difficult to consistently achieve their fundraising goals. These organizations are notorious for rapid turnover and high donor attrition, which I will argue are merely side effects of a larger problem. I believe one of the greatest opportunities for positive disruption in the nonprofit sector, especially for small shops with limited staff and resources, is a new definition of fundraising talent. This new definition is narrowly focused on raising the expectations of existing donors and becoming much less reliant on new donor acquisition. In doing so, we allow ourselves the opportunity to be recognized and admired for our own distinct and deliberate practices.

My critique is also aimed at those like me, who assist these organizations. I routinely encounter nonprofits, primarily small ones, that have been given fundraising counsel inconsistent with how fundraising can truly be effective. The greatest flaw in this advice is an emphasis on the many (donors) rather than the few. Successful fundraising is the outcome of a pinpoint strategy that engages key categories of donors in meaningful ways, beginning with those who will ultimately have the greatest impact. If the process is carried out well, no donor, regardless of the size of his gift, will receive more or less gratitude than others who give. The process is orchestrated specifically not to elevate any donor over another, but rather to ensure that a goal is successfully achieved.

In some ways, the war for fundraising talent is success favoring those who have already been successful. As the more advantaged organizations achieve greater success, they naturally attract a greater share of a limited resource, whatever it happens to be, ultimately diminishing the availability of that resource to other organizations.

As well-performing organizations find success easier, others find it increasingly difficult to avoid failure. This dynamic becomes a sort of self-fulfilling prophecy—the lauded organizations tend to become increasingly confident, with larger fundraising goals, while their discouraged counterparts hunker down in constant fear of disaster and can barely manage to keep the lights on.

This book is also intended to align fundraising professionals with nonprofit organizations that share a common commitment to highly effective fundraising practices. So, *The War for Fundraising Talent* is intended for two audiences: the aspiring fundraising professional and the organizational leaders who hire them.

For aspiring fundraising professionals, my hope is that this book will be one of the first they read, even before they accept a position. Its insights at that critical juncture in a career will cause some to reconsider whether fundraising is truly the right path for them to make an impact in the nonprofit sector. For those confident of their role, they'll be able to identify organizations that truly understand how effective fundraising really works.

Board members, nonprofit executives and major donors will find this book to be a lens that will help them evaluate their current fundraising practices as well as a standard to help them develop future practices. Alignment between the fundraising professional and organizational leaders is the only way to ensure we get fundraising right. Otherwise, fundraising professionals will continue to gravitate to the most advantaged organizations, and small shops will persist in their track record of delivering on mediocre outcomes.

While writing this book, and with a talented graphic designer (thank you, Anna), I had the opportunity to help create four training models that visually represent my fundraising philosophy. This book, combined with these four models, provides the foundation from which my colleagues and I assist nonprofit organizations in improving their fundraising capacity. The four models serve to align organizational leaders, their boards of directors, volunteers, and fundraising professionals around a shared understanding of how fundraising really works. I encourage you to familiarize yourself with the concepts, periodically return to these models, and enjoy a visual perspective of how my story and the stories of others have imbued my philosophy of effective fundraising.

The War for Fundraising Talent

I F WE WERE TO ASK nonprofit executives what their greatest challenge is in accomplishing the organization's mission, many would point to fundraising as number one. Even those with budgets large enough to employ dedicated fundraising professionals aren't spared. But the problem isn't the money itself.

The grisly reality for nonprofits is that talented fundraising professionals are in high demand—and in short supply. High demand and short supply leads to a trifecta of problems. Today's nonprofit organizations, especially those relying on charitable giving as a primary source of revenue, are finding it increasingly difficult to identify, hire, and retain qualified fundraising professionals. Locating people who share a passion and commitment to the mission while able to consistently achieve their goals makes the search even more difficult.

As overwhelming as these challenges are, I find it interesting that employment trends among fundraising professionals closely resemble the forecasts of management consultants for the last two decades. Beginning in the late 1990s, predictions warned of impending talent shortages, rapid turnover, and rising employee expectations. Much of what was forecast had less to do with the complexities of a sector or industry, difficult financial times, and demographic shifts. Instead, they reflected the effects of an evolving, market-driven workforce. And nowhere in the nonprofit sector are the effects of the market more overlooked and misunderstood than in professional fundraising.

In 1998, the world's most prestigious management consultancy, McKinsey & Company, coined the phrase "The War for Talent."[3] According to McKinsey, The War for Talent would remain a defining characteristic of the competitive landscape for decades to come. The most ill-prepared organizations were destined to experience three devastating trends:

1. Severe talent shortages
2. Consistent vacancies in critical roles
3. Skyrocketing compensation packages

These forewarnings could easily be describing the challenges of today's nonprofits. The War for Talent suggested a complete renegotiation of the terms of employment—one that turned the negotiating power over to the most-talented employees. This wasn't merely a demographic shift or shortage in particular fields. It was an evolution of the traditional employer-employee relationship, one that represented a more efficient market for talent. Companies were convinced that talent had to be their top priority. The only path to better performance—and being more competitive—was with better talent.

Much of this shift of power from employer to employee was a consequence of decisions made by companies decades earlier, which had a ripple effect throughout the economy. They basically abandoned their obligations to employees by downsizing and restructuring, in effect abolishing job security. Employees become like free agents, looking out for themselves and gaining leverage by comparing job offers. "In the new economy, the best people are the most likely to leave. Why? Because they can. And they are likely to leave

---

3 Hankin, S.M., Michaels, E.G III. "The War for Talent," *McKinsey Quarterly* (1998).

long before they've paid their dues or even paid a return on your recruiting and training investment."[4]

Whereas McKinsey's War for Talent resembles an international conflict playing out broadly across all sectors of the economy, *the war for fundraising talent* is being waged within the boundaries of the nonprofit world. The war for fundraising talent is the sector's battle with the law of supply and demand, combined with its inability to create environments where fundraising professionals can achieve mastery and find meaning in their work.

The war for fundraising talent can be won with two strategies: First, nonprofits must retain more of our existing supply of talented fundraising professionals. Second, nonprofits must empower new recruits with an understanding of how both they and their employers can achieve success.

This will require that the perks of becoming a fundraiser include more than the opportunity to receive an extraordinary compensation package and the promise of changing the world. The sector has an obligation to tip the scales so there are more places where fundraisers can find success. Organizations of all shapes and sizes must share a common understanding of how effective fundraising really works. Increasing the supply of fundraisers without ensuring adequate return-on-investment for every organization only complicates our problems.

This inter-sector conflict is especially perplexing when you consider the two camps that differ in understanding what effective fundraising really looks like. Their unique perspectives comprise subtle differences of opinion regarding the resources they're fighting for. One camp recognizes that any *lack of talent* becomes the primary disadvantage; the other camp believes the *lack of donors with dollars* is always the scarcest resource.

---

4 Tulgan, B. *Winning the Talent Wars* (WW Norton and Company, New York, 2001).

Consequently, the latter camp would not be inclined to embrace the premise of this book, preferring a solution that better aligns with its definition of the problem. Those open to this premise stand to gain valuable insight and strategies that will help their fundraisers and organizations thrive.

All this amounts to an ideological debate over how nonprofits grow and thrive; one camp tends toward attracting talent because of its understanding of effective fundraising. This camp seeks the advantages of a mature fundraising operation with talented individuals who can consistently achieve their goals. In contrast, the other camp has inherited a learned helplessness and loyalty to a system designed to fail them and their missions.

The Magnetic Workplace

In many ways, the challenges for fundraising professionals resemble those of the nursing field, where it's thought that shortages can be easily remedied by attracting new talent. Despite the healthcare industry's efforts at making nursing a more attractive career option, those already in the field understand one thing quite well—that merely increasingly the supply of nurses only complicates matters until more systemic problems are addressed.

As Gordon Lafer, political economist and former Senior Labor Policy Advisor for the US Congress, explains, "There is not an actual shortage of nurses at this point. Instead, there is a shortage of nurses willing to work under the conditions currently offered by the hospital industry."[5] Similarly, the fundraising profession doesn't have a shortage of enthusiastic people willing

---

5   Lafer, G. "Hospital Speedups and the Fiction of a Nursing Shortage," *Labor Studies Journal*, 30, Issue 1: 27–46.

and able to raise funds for organizations they care about. The supply of fundraising talent is limited by a growing unwillingness on their part to tolerate conditions that interfere with their ability to achieve mastery and find meaning in their work.

Lafer says the current nursing shortage is the result of industry decisions made in the 1990s like those that McKinsey's research pointed out: Reductions in the nursing staff. Increases in patient loads. A near-freeze in average wages. These decisions led to consistent factors that influenced nurses in making the decision to resign.

Because of how it handled this, the healthcare industry essentially created quite a predicament for itself. Their efforts to reduce costs have come back to haunt them. Likewise, nonprofit organizations have a track record of making fundraising-related decisions that routinely return to haunt them. Efforts to raise funds are held to a model that results in an experience for both the fundraising professional and donor that is less than meaningful.

The good news is there's hope for both the nursing profession and the fundraising profession. Research shows there's a direct correlation between the patient experience and the quality of the nurse's experience as a hospital employee. One way of measuring how a nurse experiences the workplace is through the Magnet Recognition Program, created by the American Nurses Credentialing Center. Magnet hospitals receive their designation through an objective evaluation of the nursing experience. Research indicates that the magnet hospitals themselves experience several advantages, including higher net income, reductions in nursing turnover, and lower mortality rates. [6]

Although lacking any official designation, some nonprofit organizations are recognized as magnets for great

---

6 Stimpfel, A. W., Sloane, D. M., McHugh, M. D. and Aiken, L. H. "Hospitals Known for Nursing Excellence Associated with Better Hospital Experience for Patients" *Health Services Research* (2016).

fundraising talent, and others deserve to be recognized as such. Unfortunately, there are others that, despite their best intentions, have an organizational culture that repels success in fundraising. What's troubling is that these organizations are not necessarily aware of their inherent weaknesses. Worse, few in the sector have the courage to proactively assist them with identifying and addressing these weaknesses. While many fundraising professionals are aware of their organization's flaws, rather than attempting to confront the leadership, they find it easier to resign, hoping to have more success elsewhere.

With many fundraising professionals failing to commit to staying in fundraising, the instability within the fundraising profession is quite clear. Forty percent of development directors said fundraising was their current field of work, but they weren't sure they would stay in it for their entire careers. This was significantly more common among fundraisers at small- and mid-sized organizations.[7]

To lessen the instability, we must understand the terrain through which today's fundraisers must traverse. The opportunities and challenges are very different than those of a generation ago. Today's fundraising professionals are increasingly aware of the inherent dysfunction that interferes with their ability to succeed. They also recognize their chosen career path is still earning its legitimacy among the public, and that its foundation remains dependent on other professional fields. Despite the challenges, these professionals recognize the growing list of opportunities that await them wherever they go.

---

7   Bell, J., Cornelius, M. *UnderDeveloped: A National Study of Challenges Facing Nonprofit Fundraising* (CompassPoint Nonprofit Services and the Evelyn and Walter Haas, Jr. Fund, San Francisco, 2013).

Inheriting Dysfunction

In research funded by the Anne E. Casey Foundation, Francis Kunreuther and Patrick Convington challenge the dominant theme of crisis associated with the baby boomer exodus from the nonprofit sector. They say the next generation of nonprofit executives is not inclined to accept the sector as is, that it will need to address broad structural issues rather than simply filling the leadership pipeline. [8]

New leaders are aware of the overwhelming job descriptions of many executive directors, the limits of nonprofit compensation, and funders' unrealistic expectations that starve organizations of critical resources. For their part, fundraising professionals see how organizational design and culture interferes with their ability to succeed. While no organization is immune to its share of messiness, nonprofits are especially tolerant of some habits and behaviors that undermine fundraising effectiveness.

Many nonprofit organizations exist in a culture of dysfunction—a dysfunction that pervades strategic planning, staffing, training, management, financing, and performance measurement.[9] This dysfunction explains why many younger nonprofit leaders are reluctant to assume the posts being vacated by today's retiring baby boomers. These up-and-coming leaders are asking themselves whether, and to what extent, they will assume responsibility for the sector's dysfunction. And while the dysfunction affects all aspects of the organization, they recognize that fundraising is at the top of the list.

---

8 The Annie E. Casey Foundation. *Next Shift: Beyond the Nonprofit Leadership Crisis*. Baltimore: (The Annie E. Casey Foundation, 2007). http://www.aecf.org/m/resourcedoc/AECF-NextShift-2008-Full.pdf. Accessed November 8, 2017.

9 Community Wealth Ventures. *Venture Philanthropy: Landscape and Expectations*. (The Morino Institute, 2000)

According to a recent study, the number one—and unsurprising—finding was that the sector is on the verge of losing large numbers of leaders. Especially relevant was the second key finding, the cycle of frustration fundraising creates for nonprofit leaders, one they're increasingly cognizant of and unwilling to inherit.[10] The fundraising responsibilities expected of many executive directors are incompatible with the remainder of their job descriptions.

Hidden dysfunctional mindsets affect decisions about compensation in our sector, deliberately keeping wages low. Paying a person more, so one theory goes, increases the likelihood his employment is financially, rather than mission motivated.[11] Historically, nurses and teachers have encountered this same wage differential based on the assumption that an underpaid employee performs better because of his dedication. Valid or not, these theories hold water only if the supply of intrinsically-motivated employees exceeds the demand.

Early in their careers, fundraising professionals discover that expecting a competitive wage is interpreted as having motives that are less than honorable. The response to a request for a more competitive salary is often followed by an accusation of prioritizing money over mission. The accuser typically has little understanding of the effects of a labor market for highly skilled employees. He fails to consider that nonprofits offer compelling mission statements regardless of what they're paying.

Today's nonprofits, especially those that rely mainly on charitable giving, find it increasingly difficult to identify, hire,

10 http://tsne.org/downloads/Leadership_New_England_Report_TSNE. pdf. Accessed November 8, 2017.

11 Leete, L. "Work in the Nonprofit Sector" in: Powell, W.W., Steinberg R. (Eds.), *The NonProfit Sector. A Research Handbook* (Yale University Press, New Haven/London, 2006).

and retain qualified fundraising professionals. By insisting on a lower-than-market wage for fundraisers, nonprofits risk the very effectiveness of their own organization.

In his provocative book, *Uncharitable*, Dan Pallotta insists the sector's compensation theories are the number one error undermining its effectiveness. The sector believes it must limit compensation to some arbitrary threshold based on emotion and "gut feelings," and it does so for fear of moving fully into the free market.[12] Hiring a fundraising professional can be the first place where new executives and new board members encounter the reality that fear, emotion and gut feelings no longer work. By the time they begin competing to hire talented fundraisers in an increasingly competitive market, they're aware of the way arbitrary caps interfere with their goals.

No research demonstrating the sector's dysfunctional relationships with its benefactors has received more attention than "The Nonprofit Starvation Cycle."[13] This research highlights the tendency of nonprofits to keep overhead expenses artificially low to compete with other charities for charitable dollars. This persistently underfunds the non-mission-related structure of the nonprofit. By misrepresenting the notorious line item, "overhead," to demonstrate how much of the funds go directly to "the work," nonprofits cut off their own circulation. Worse, they teach donors that their nonprofit needs *even less money* to continue to carry out its mission. Thus, the starvation cycle gathers momentum, as donors expect nonprofits to function on ever-less money, while somehow accomplishing even more.

If the vicious cycle remains unchanged, funders' expectations about what it takes to run a nonprofit continue to shrink, as does

---

12 Pallotta, D. *Uncharitable: How Restraints on Nonprofits Undermine Their Potential* (Tufts University Press, 2010).

13 Goggins-Gregory, A. & Howard, D. "The Nonprofit Starvation Cycle" *Stanford Social Innovation Review* (2009).

their giving. The nonprofit is then forced to somehow shave even more from administrative or infrastructure costs, thereby lessening its own effectiveness. In turn, it is unable to invest enough money in the organization to function optimally and make significant, measurable gains in its mission.

Turning this cycle around begins with re-educating donors about what it takes to run a nonprofit, basically changing how we all raise money. The starvation cycle demands that organizations fundamentally change how they communicate their needs. We must replace an overreliance on arm's-length communication, often characterized by nothing more than written proposals, with a commitment to more meaningful interaction.

Growing into Our Own

In November 2012, Robert Phillips shocked the PR industry when he resigned as EMEA president and CEO of Edelman, the world's largest PR company. News of Phillips' resignation came just two weeks after it was announced he'd been tasked with a global initiative to ensure the firm remained at the forefront of public relations innovation. In his book, *Trust Me, PR is Dead*, Phillips describes a conversation he'd had a month earlier with his friend and boss Richard Edelman.

Phillips shared strong concerns about their industry: their unwillingness to embrace data, a preference for generalists rather than mastery, and a focus on corporate growth instead of on developing the skillsets and intelligence necessary to better serve their clients. Despite his agreement with Phillips' concerns, Edelman said their model couldn't change; it would take too long and cause too much disruption. Phillips writes: ". . . [I]t was there and then I decided to quit. I could not be a hypocrite. I felt like an imposter."[141]

---

14 Phillips, R. *Trust Me, PR Is Dead* (Random House, UK, 2015).

Just a few months before Phillips' resignation, Bill Lee had declared in the *Harvard Business Review*, "Traditional marketing—including advertising, public relations, branding and corporate communications—is dead." Lee warned that many working in these fields were unaware that they were operating within a dead paradigm.[15] More recently, Ken Burnett, the author of *Relationship Fundraising* and a marketer turned fundraising expert, concluded after several decades that marketing was not a good fit for fundraising.[16]

Whether we agree with these bold assertions is not as important as our willingness to examine the foundations on which our profession has been built. If marketing and PR are experiencing a mid-life crisis, the fundraising profession is only working its way through the messy adolescent years. It's questionable how much longer the fundraising profession can continue to rely on the foundations of marketing and public relations.

> *Fundraising is a maturing profession, but one that is increasingly controversial. Media reports of poor practice have contributed to concerns about the integrity of fundraisers and the uses which have been made of the resources they raise. As a result, a consensus now exists among senior figures in the industry about the changes that are required. Technique is no longer enough. Many more of the next generation of practitioners must be capable of considered reflection, organizational and inter-organizational strategic thinking, and value-based leadership.[17]*
>
> Thoughtful Fundraising,
> *editors Jill Mordaunt and Rob Paton*

---

15 Lee, B. "Marketing Is Dead" *Harvard Business Review* (2012).

16 Burnett, K. "Marketing Was a Mistake" http://www.kenburnett.com/Blog54Marketingwasamistake.htm. Accessed November, 8, 2017.

17 *Thoughtful Fundraising: Concepts, Issues, and Perspectives*, ed. Mourdaunt, J., Paton, R. (New York: Routledge, 2007).

Clearly, change is needed. But who will guide this change? In 2011, thirty-five influential leaders from across the nonprofit sector gathered in Washington, DC for the nation's first Growing Philanthropy Summit. This highly influential group declared the sector remains overly focused on donor acquisition. Participants suggested a misunderstanding of "relationship building" was at fault, while others blamed a seriously flawed business model.

> *Most of the fundraising industry operates on a business model that pays by volumes of pieces mailed, phone calls made, and online impressions garnered. So agencies are compensated by quantities of solicitation and not by the quality of donor base that results. It's a business model that affects donor file churn. This will not change until buyers' minds are informed and changed.*[18]

Today's fundraising talent will need to have the courage of Phillips and Lee, who declared their professions dead, and Burnett, who has evidently examined his own assumptions and declared marketing as wrong for fundraising. We'll need to acknowledge that our profession is growing up, take responsibility for ourselves and our practices, and learn to stand on our own two feet.

Exporting Talent

In today's nonprofit sector, many fail to recognize the tug of opportunities that tempt fundraising professionals away from their current employers. Talented fundraising professionals are discovering that some organizations do offer visible advantages

---

18 www.blackbaud.com/files/resources/downloads/WhitePaper_ GrowingPhilanthropyReport_Summary.pdf. Accessed November 8, 2017.

that can help ensure immediate success and further develop their own fundraising abilities. Even before an initial interview, a candidate can easily investigate whether a prospective employer can provide the elements that typically drive highly effective fundraising: a solid constituency, infrastructure, and track record.

Larger metropolitan areas home to national and international organizations have always served as gravitational pulls for nonprofit employees. A large subset of nonprofit employees already works for "anchor institutions," large, urban powerhouses which offer a concentration of resources, influence, and talent. These anchors are the Google-plexes of the nonprofit sector. They often have impressive fundraising operations and can serve as launching pads for rewarding fundraising careers.

But here's the thing: these larger institutions are no longer confined within US borders. The nonprofit sector is becoming increasingly global, and the fundraising profession always rides along on its coattails. While the local nonprofit employer has historically worried about a nearby nonprofit—or worse, a large national organization in a major US city—poaching its fundraising talent, an increasing number of opportunities are becoming available to American fundraising professionals who want to work abroad. Gone are the days when a promising major gifts officer leaves to work at the nearby university; instead, he may be accepting an offer in, say, Australia.

In addition to the opportunities around the world, there is tension between beginning a career at a larger nonprofit versus at a smaller organization. High-profile thought leaders insist, "Do not go to a small organization under any circumstances. Small organizations don't have a lot of know-how or systems or support . . . [and] have a severe lack of understanding about what it takes to be successful."[19] Leaders at the California Community Foundation characterize this tension as the major giving wars between large educational and healthcare institutions. They point out that, in Los Angeles, the two fundraising powerhouses (USC and UCLA) have a staff of more than 750 fundraising professionals. The magnitude of talent consolidated within these two organizations makes it especially difficult for smaller shops to compete.[20]

Rise of Donor Intent

The most challenging terrain for today's fundraising professionals may be the conflict between their employer's fear of mission drift and their donors' insistence that the organization honor their charitable intent. The rise of donor intent, from sun-setting foundations to donor-advised funds and even crowdfunding, is a clear message that donors want their intentions clearly understood and honored.

The conflict between mission drift and donor intent is highlighted in a 2016 report warning that unprecedented levels of charitable giving mask an alarming trend: Charities are relying on larger and grander donations from smaller numbers of high-income, high-wealth donors. As most fundraising professionals are quick to point out, this trend aligns with a shift in organizational fundraising strategies that prioritize major donors.[21] This change in strategy is an attempt to raise more money while expending

---

19 Lindsay, D. "Big vs. Little" *The Chronicle of Philanthropy* (July 06, 2016).

20 www.huffingtonpost.com/john-e-kobara/the-new-normal-mega-donors-and-fewer-recipients_b_7672790.html. Accessed November 8, 2017.

21 www.ips-dc.org/wp-content/uploads/2016/11/Gilded-Giving-Final-pdf. Accessed March 2017.

the same, or less, cost. The only way to accomplish this goal is for nonprofits to focus on fewer and larger donors.

The same report showed that nonprofit revenues from donors at lower- and middle-income levels are shrinking. From 2003 to 2013, charitable deductions from donors making less than $100,000 *declined by 34 percent*. The fear is that relying on fewer, major donors could shift the work of individual nonprofits—or even the entire sector—toward an agenda governed by the elite. To prevent this, the study said organizations need to protect themselves (and their missions) from the increasing influence of large-scale, mega donations. Fundraising professionals will interpret this as a catch-22; raising more money at fixed or lower costs without increasing reliance on larger donors is simply impossible.

While traditional nonprofits may be receiving larger but fewer gifts, and smaller donors may not be responding to traditional fundraising methods, these smaller donors may be giving in ways that are more consistent with their personal interests and preferences and not all that inconsistent with their wealthy counterparts.

In 2016, the crowdfunding site GoFundMe reached a major milestone: $3 billion in funding contributions since its founding. These funds were contributed by more than 20 million people donating 30 million times to two million different GoFundMe campaigns.[22] According to the Pew Research Center, the most popular kinds of crowdfunding projects are contributions to help someone in need. Many donations in this fast-growing category are not tax-deductible—and therefore off the radar for think tanks to analyze.[23] Whereas we have historically expected smaller and

---

22 medium.com/@Robsolomon1/gofundme-hits-2-billion-raised-55e119a751f0#.59yk419g2. Accessed March 2017.

23 www.pewinternet.org/2016/05/19/the-new-digital-economy/pi_2016-05-19_sharing-economy_4-04/. Accessed March 2017.

mid-range donors to follow our lead, today they are discovering that new tools enable them to give as they wish.

Susan Ostrander notes philanthropy has shifted heavily to the supply side in the last two decades, toward a relationship dynamic controlled more and more by the donor. She points to the growth of donor-advised funds (DAFs) as one place where the donor is "becoming closely involved in highly directive ways in the organizations they support. . . . All of these trends increase the prominence and authority of wealthy donors in philanthropy." [24] While DAFs date to the Great Depression, their expanded use today reflects the determination of donors to make a more informed, strategic and timely gift. DAFs afford the donor all the tax benefits of a charitable gift without imposing any immediate obligation for its use.

In 1991, Fidelity Investments established its own Charitable Gift Fund, which has since become an entire industry.[25] By 2000, investors could put money in DAFs held at Vanguard, Schwab, Oppenheimer, and J.P. Morgan Chase. In 2016, Fidelity's Charitable Gift Fund surpassed the United Way by receiving nearly a billion dollars more in contributions.[26] For most of us in the nonprofit sector, donor-advised funds have become a place where donor contributions are not just stored, but they have also created a channel through which we anticipate charitable gifts. That year, Fidelity ranked number two in grant-making, trailing only behind the Gates Foundation.[272]

---

24 Ostrander, S. *The Growth of Donor Control: Revisiting the Social Relations of Philanthropy* (Tufts University). Downloaded from nvs.sagepub.com at Pennsylvania State Univ on May 16, 2016, accessed March 2017.

25 www.fidelitycharitable.org. Accessed November 8, 2017.

26 www.philanthropy.com/article/Fidelity-Charitable-Knocks/238167. Accessed March 2017.

27 Frank, R. "Second biggest charitable giver? Fidelity Donor Fund" www.cnbc.com/2015/06/10/second-biggest-charitable-giver-fidelity-donor-

Despite its attractiveness to donors, the DAF has its critics. Some argue that DAFs are undermining the ability of nonprofits to generate the critical resources they need now. To be fair, accumulating charitable gifts for future use is something private foundations have always afforded the wealthy. Just as DAF managers may be motivated to retain assets (to collect fees and accumulate investment earnings), private foundations tend to capitalize on these same opportunities. Perhaps most critical is that donor-advised funds basically democratize philanthropy, making it possible for the middle class to give more deliberately as well.

On the opposite end of the charitable gift spectrum, GoFundMe's CEO estimates it will generate at least $40 billion in the next decade: "We want to reach a place where we are doing more than the largest organizations and foundations in the world." He says the philanthropy of the future delivers money faster, more democratically, and with fewer contingencies, and that GoFundMe is "committed to being the best place for people to help each other on our way to being the largest giving organization in the world."[28] While DAFs may result in more intentional, significant gifts, and crowdfunding may reflect more-impulsive and generally trivial gifts, both channels point toward a donor who is digging in her heels and insisting charitable giving be done *on her own terms*.

Today's fundraising professionals are discovering they may soon be able to raise funds on their own terms as well, in ways that don't feel manipulative or inauthentic, and that honor the donor's intent without potentially violating the organization's mission statement. McKinsey was right when they observed

---

fund.html. Accessed November 8, 2017

28 www.fastcoexist.com/3066778/future-of-philanthropy/gofundmes-biggest-cause-yet-is-becoming-the-most-powerful-force-in-ph. Accessed March 2017.

that the war for talent completely renegotiated the terms of employment, turning the negotiating power over to the most talented employees. With new terms, fundraisers can begin to model for their employers how effective fundraising really works and ensure that they are recognized and admired for practices that ensure positive change.

Hounded by Charities

I N THE FALL OF 2014, Olive Cooke explained to the *Bristol Post* that, in just one month, she had received 267 appeal letters from nonprofits asking for her support. In addition to her regular mail, Olive said she regularly received *up to ten solicitation letters every single day*. She told the *Post*, "I open and read every single one of them, but my problem is I've always been one that reads about the cause, and I can't say no. The stories play on people's generosity."[29]

In the past she'd given to some of the organizations asking for her support, yet there were others she'd never given to. She assumed some of the organizations must have sold her details to others, which would explain the rising tide of requests.

Six months later, Olive Cooke's body was found in the Avon Gorge, a canyon on the River Avon in Bristol, England. The headlines said Olive Cooke had committed suicide after being hounded by charities. Her family insisted that depression was a more likely explanation. Yet the press had already made up its mind: greedy nonprofit organizations and their poor fundraising practices were to blame. Olive's family wanted her to be remembered as kind, generous, charitable, and "a strong believer in the importance of charities." Unfortunately, Olive Cooke will be remembered far less for her many years of service and generosity and more for the impact her death had on the fundraising profession.

---

29 www.dailymail.co.uk/news/article-3081294/Britain-s-oldest-poppy-seller-dead-Avon-Gorge-aged-92.html. Accessed April 2017.

Following Olive's death, the UK's now-defunct Fundraising Standards Board (FRSB) was asked to investigate the fundraising practices believed to have contributed to this tragic event. Andrew Hind, chair of the FRSB, described the situation as "the inevitable consequences of a fundraising regime where charities have been willing to exchange or sell the personal details of donors to each other and to commercial third parties." In the FRSB report, Hind suggested that the individual charities had no way of knowing the cumulative impact of their practices, nor how many other organizations might be approaching Mrs. Cooke at any given time.[30]

The report showed Olive was regularly contributing to forty-eight charities.[31] Despite her generous intentions, Olive was contributing to a process designed to break even at best. Olive was unaware that the costs of new donor acquisition had risen so high in recent years that they basically offset any meaningful impact her contributions might have had. Without being asked to upgrade her level of giving or voluntarily deciding to do so—which presumably would have required that she consolidate her giving to fewer charities—her contributions were essentially a loss.

Who is to Blame?

When a system doesn't seem to be working, it's human nature to go looking for someone to blame. In the public forum, Olive was the victim of the greedy charities that wanted to extract every last dime in her pocket. However, some would blame Olive for failing to understand how fundraising really works. Compelled

---

30 https://fundraising.co.uk/2016/01/20/frsb-publishes-results-of-olive-cooke-investigation-and-related-complaint. Accessed April 2017.

31 Ibid.

to support every charity that comes knocking, donors like Olive scatter their charitable giving so thinly it has little impact. Their compulsiveness and inability to say no signals an unwillingness or incapacity to make more-significant commitments, whether this is true or not. The charities, in turn, tend to rely on the most efficient, impersonal fundraising methods to sustain the relationship: what I refer to as arm's-length fundraising.

The tragedy of Olive Cooke isn't simply that of direct mail fundraising gone amuck. And while direct mail is a usual suspect, the tragedy points to the sector's addiction to any fundraising method that deceives its users into believing that by continuously increasing the volume of trivial gifts exchanged at arm's length, it can sustain an organization's mission. The seeds of this addiction began after World War II, when large nonprofits in the US discovered that direct mail was especially efficient in raising large sums. In fact, it worked so well that these organizations often deposited the money without keeping a record of where it came from. Rather than tempt fate, they sent out identical appeals to the same addresses the following year.[32]

To characterize any gift as trivial is heart-wrenching for some fundraising professionals. "Every gift counts," they insist. These eternal optimists want to believe every gift they receive reflects a deep commitment to the organization and a priority spot in their donor's checkbook. Ironically, many of these same fundraisers are active contributors to a system that never allows them the opportunity to learn whether a gift is trivial or not. The system deliberately minimizes the intimacy that would afford them the opportunity to ask such an honest question.

---

32 Warwick , M. *Revolution in the Mailbox: Your Guide to Successful Direct Mail Fundraising (The Mal Warwick Fundraising Series)* (Jossey-Bass (Wiley), San Francisco, 2004).

Direct mail for new donor acquisition isn't necessarily a bad idea, nor would it be fair to label this in itself as an addiction. An addiction to arm's-length fundraising evolves when organizations continue to use channels of communication best reserved for first-time gifts in their attempts to renew and upgrade support. Once an initial gift has been received, the relationship has changed and both sides of the relationship will have higher expectations of the other. As they move forward, their actions should reflect this, but they often don't. As a major donor once told me, "They keep asking me for larger checks and offering the same shallow relationship in return."

Instead of owning up to their preference for cheap fundraising, organizations rationalize their behavior by differentiating between appeals designed for a first-time gift and those designed for continued support, yet the appeals remain fundamentally the same. A few donors will tolerate the impersonal appeal in exchange for the warm glow of "changing the world." The majority will not; the sector is well-aware that upwards of three-fourths of first-time gifts will not be renewed the following year. According to the Fundraising Effectiveness Study, every 100 donors gained in 2016 was offset by 99 in donors lost through attrition. Translating this into dollars, every $100 gained in 2016 was offset by $95 in losses through gift attrition. You can't change the world with this type of track record. Yet some in our sector refuse to consider that the system is broken.[33]

One of the mistaken assumptions of arm's-length fundraising is that an organization can maintain meaningful relationships with its donors without acknowledging them as individuals. In doing so, they routinely draw broad-brush conclusions about their donors' feelings—what they will appreciate, find

---

33 http://afpfep.org/wp-content/uploads/2017/04/FEP2017Report4212017. pdf. Accessed November 9, 2017.

meaningful, or respond favorably to. Economists refer to this assumption as *the fallacy of collective terms*, meaning we expect a group to behave in the same manner as an individual. As one economist pointed out, "[We] recognize that the only living, breathing, thinking, and acting entity is the individual. The source of all human action is the individual. Others may acquiesce . . . or even participate, but everything which occurs as a consequence can be traced to particular, identifiable individuals." Economists warn that when people grow weary of the collective terms, they leave in search of another group with more attractive terms.[34]

The subtle appeal of arm's-length fundraising is its ability to guard both sides of the exchange from the uncomfortable feelings that accompany charitable giving. It prevents those of us who are donors or fundraisers from confronting the underlying psychology in our motives, our philosophies of giving and receiving gifts, and the life experiences that influence our decisions. The greater the distance maintained in the relationship, literally or figuratively, the easier it is for a donor to refuse a request. Likewise, this makes it easier for the fundraiser to avoid his hesitancy in asking and fear of rejection. Unfortunately, if the connection runs like a complicated machine rather than like interactions between living, breathing human beings, fundraising is sapped of the generosity and gratitude that make it a uniquely human experience.

Some organizations are quite content with their complicated machines, and for them, change is too risky. They've managed to accumulate such an enormous mailing list that, for the time being, they can overcome the realities of rising costs, unsubstantial gifts and donor attrition by turning up the knob

---

34 Reed, LW. *7 Fallacies of Economics* (Foundation for Economic Education, 1981). https://fee.org/articles/7-fallacies-of-economics. Accessed April 2017.

on the weary few who continue to give at arm's length. Let's just hope no one else jumps off a bridge.

These organizations don't recognize that it is the nature of machinery to either break down or become obsolete. Systems that break down are expensive to fix; when they become obsolete, the process must start all over again. The fundamental solution is to first recognize our sector's addiction to fundraising without meaningful relationships that in turn bars us from expecting and receiving meaningful levels of support. To better understand an organizational dependency on arm's-length fundraising, let's consider how contemporary research has improved our understanding of addiction.

Trapped in a Cage

After his professional career as a journalist imploded amidst allegations of plagiarism, Johann Hari needed an opportunity to start over. Rather than sulk in his misery and risk the chance of developing his own addictions to mask the shame and embarrassment of his mistakes, Hari began a three-and-a-half-year journey to understand the underlying causes of addiction. In his book, *Chasing the Scream*, Hari recalls, as a child, being unable to waken his relatives from a drunken stupor.[35] His journey culminated in a 2015 TED Talk with him noting, "the opposite of addiction is not sobriety. The opposite of addiction is connection."[36]

To his surprise, Hari discovered nearly everything he thought he knew about addiction was based on myth, and that

---

35 Hari, J. *Chasing the Scream, the First and the Last Days on the War on Drugs* (Bloomsbury USA, New York, 2015).

36 https://www.ted.com/talks/johann_hari_everything_you_think_you_know_about_addiction_is_wrong. Accessed November 9, 2017.

much of the science we've come to rely on in the last century to explain it is wrong. One of his most enlightening discoveries came via Dr. Bruce Alexander, a psychologist who has researched addiction since 1970 in British Columbia, Canada.[37]

Beginning in the 1960s, scientists used rats, monkeys, and other laboratory animals to test addiction theories. The monkeys were restrained to a chair with a button that would administer the drug, while rats were placed in isolated cages and given two water bottles to choose from. One contained morphine; the other did not. In most cases, the animals would administer the drug to the point of death. The scientists concluded these drugs must have some extraordinary power that rendered its users' incapable of resisting the temptation for more. Their conclusions continue to influence legislation that regulates and prohibits drug use today.[38]

Alexander believed these "exposure" theories of addiction were fundamentally flawed. One of the questions he raised was about the cage: "Strapping a monkey into a chair for days on end, and giving it a button to push for relief, says nothing about the power of drugs and everything about the power of restraints— social, physical, and psychological."[39] To debunk the exposure theories, Alexander and his colleagues designed a series of experiments, now famously known as "Rat Park." Rather than using an isolated cage, they designed a large plywood enclosure in which rats could freely interact, play, and mate. The rats were given food and two water bottles to choose from. Again, one contained morphine; the other did not. The results were just as eye-opening as Dr. Alexander's team had predicted: In an environment where dependency wasn't necessary for survival,

---

37 Hari, *Chasing the Scream.*

38 Slater, L. *Opening Skinner's Box: Great Psychological Experiments of the Twentieth Century* (W.W. Norton & Co., New York, 2004)

39 Ibid.

the rats had no need for drugs. The rats in Rat Park were far less likely to gravitate to the drug-induced water. In his interviews with Dr. Alexander, Hari discovered drugs hadn't cause the harmful behavior he observed as a child; the environment had.[40] Hari concluded, "An isolated rat will almost always become a junkie. A rat with a good life almost never will, no matter how many drugs you make available to him."[41]

In over four decades of addiction research, Dr. Alexander concluded that: 1) addiction is not a consequence of overexposure to powerful substances; and 2) its definition must extend beyond drugs and alcohol to other dangerous and destructive patterns and habits. According to Alexander, addiction is a narrowly focused lifestyle that functions as a meager substitute for what psychologists refer to as psychosocial integration. This term describes the interdependence that develops between individuals and society, which balances their need for social belonging with their need for autonomy and achievement. Alternative names for this include social cohesion, community, and belonging. Dislocation is the opposite—social isolation, alienation, and disconnection.[42]

In the rush to declare Olive Cooke the victim of greedy nonprofits, no one dared suggest she and the organizations she was supporting were merely trapped in a cage, both addicted to meager substitutes for meaningful relationships. For her part, Olive was unaware she was providing so little support to each organization that it necessitated the most efficient methods of exchange—eliminating any chance of a meaningful connection.

---

40 Hari, J. *Chasing the Scream, the First and the Last Days on the War on Drugs* (Bloomsbury USA, New York, 2015)

41 https://www.ted.com/talks/johann_hari_everything_you_think_you_know_about_addiction_is_wrong.

42 Alexander, B. *The Globalization of Addiction: A Study in Poverty of the Spirit* (Oxford University Press, New York, 2008).

Equally disturbing, the organizations neglected to consider the implications of a system that exploited the naïve and misinformed. Ian MacQuillin, at Plymouth University's Centre for Sustainable Fundraising, explained that after her death, they discovered that Olive regularly gave to far more charities than the average person did—several standard deviations away from the mean.[43] Her giving habits were unusual, yet none of the organizations had the audacity to ask why giving to so many organizations was necessary. Nor did anyone question whether the root of this behavior lay in something more disturbing. Olive was desperately grasping for meaning and connection, and no one had the decency to give it to her.

Instead of being a part of a healthy relationship, Olive—and her partners at nearly a hundred charities—were contributing to a dysfunctional system. Everyone was bound to a cheap, quick, low-risk and shallow approach to fundraising: what MacQuillin referred to as the "cheap acquisition mindset of charity fundraising."[44] This cheap fundraising offers the organization all the advantages that make new acquisition such an attractive approach. At the same time, it sows the seeds of a future addiction, one that carries with it the potential to undermine every new relationship it creates.

The relationship between a charitable organization and a donor can embody psychosocial integration. Unfortunately, many of today's nonprofits have failed to integrate their donors into the culture of their organizations. Yet they rely on these same individuals for their financial support. Instead of feeling valued for their contributions, donors can experience every additional request as exploitation. Realistically, that's exactly what complex machines are designed to do—to exploit value as efficiently as possible to

---

43 http://blogs.plymouth.ac.uk/criticalfundraising/2015/06/01/opinion-how-the-olive-cooke-tragedy-affects-fundraising-ethics-and-self-regualtion/. Accessed November 9, 2017.

44 Ibid.

increase profit margins. Hardly the language any charity is likely to include in its next appeal letter.

Yet donors are not the only ones exploited by this dysfunctional system. Many fundraising professionals have developed a professional identity that is entrenched in arm's-length fundraising. They insist on using practices that consistently undermine their performance and erode their opportunities for a more rewarding career.

Within many organizations, these professionals discover what it means to be dislocated. They are often isolated from the mission, characterized as a necessary evil, and mandated to maintain cheap relationships with their donors. Regardless of their efforts, they become Dr. Alexander's definition of addicts as well, as they "cling to their addictions with grim resolution, despite the harm that follows. Often, they flatly deny the harm, despite the most obvious evidence."[45]

Any organization of any size or purpose can develop an addiction to arm's-length fundraising. However, this dysfunctional system has far greater implications for small shops with limited means to hide their addiction and buffer themselves from its effects. Large or small, these organizations have created a cage for themselves, restrained to a culture characterized by cheap, quick, shallow and low-risk fundraising.

Cheap

The nonprofit sector notoriously relies on efficiency as a primary, if not sole, indicator of superior performance. This is especially true for fundraising. Author Dan Pallotta describes the simplicity of measuring fundraising efficiency (aka cheap)

---

45 Alexander. *The Globalization of Addiction.*

as an addiction in and of itself.[46] Amidst the overwhelming complexity of the nonprofit world, we crave a simple metric for evaluating our fundraising efforts. The ratio of dollars in to dollars in return couldn't be simpler.

The error in this thinking reveals itself when we apply real numbers to the equation. For example, if an organization raises $100,000 and spends $10,000, their fundraising efficiency is 90%. This level of efficiency is often celebrated with much applause. However, if the original goal was to raise $200,000 for a much-needed program or service in the community regardless of the cost of fundraising, the efforts have failed. Here again, the utility of a single measure like fundraising efficiency allows an organization to deny failure. While efficiency matters, it doesn't answer the most important questions that ensure we're achieving our goals. A preference for cheap fundraising without prioritizing effectiveness often means that needs are not being met.

Quick

Nonprofit organizations generally have two modes of operation: reactive and proactive. A reactive organization often demands immediate revenue from its fundraising efforts to address whatever urgent need or crisis it is confronting at the time. In these nonprofits, putting out the latest fire is praised, while having the foresight to prevent one from starting is overlooked. In an organizational culture where the tyranny of the urgent dominates, it becomes nearly impossible to plan effectively. Like Robin Hood taking from the rich to give to the poor, organizational leaders enjoy the adrenaline high of rescuing the organization from near disaster.

---

46 Pallotta. *Uncharitable.*

Once again, let's say an organization has a goal of raising $200,000, yet finds itself only raising half that. Savvy donors see through the crisis and instead see lack of planning, financial mismanagement and the likelihood that their support will only contribute to sustaining a vicious cycle. The nonprofit asks for immediate cash gifts to keep the doors open and lights on rather than a well-planned and informed gift that aligns with the long-term strategic goals of the organization. Rather than confront the apparent dysfunction in crisis appeals, donors hedge their compassion by responding with trivial gifts, hoping that, together with others' contributions, the organizations will stave off whatever impending crisis looms this time.

Low Risk

Just as children mature into adults, healthy organizations eventually mature through experiences that develop their confidence even in unfamiliar territory. An organization that is especially averse to risk comes to believe that arm's-length fundraising is the safest way to avoid any risk they assume comes with more-significant donors. In this way, nonprofits maintain a clear distance between the money we must have and the mission we must protect at all costs. The risks of losing control, along with rejection or failure, often compel organizations to design their fundraising efforts to minimize these possibilities. The explicit goal of raising money becomes secondary to the implicit goal of avoiding whatever they fear the most.

Taking a closer look at the $200,000 example where only $100,000 was raised, it's easy to discover that there could be several implicit motives behind the strategy. We could have relied on capable volunteers, but instead our strategy was heavily dependent on paid staff. The risk that volunteers might fail to meet our expectations necessitates paid employees that we supposedly can count on. Rather than target fewer donors in anticipation of more meaningful gifts, we use a broad approach to avoid risking higher expectations from our donors. We could have evaluated our performance based on effectiveness, yet we chose efficiency. Clearly, risk avoidance is at the heart of this dysfunctional model. The underlying risk that organizational leaders tend to fear most—that of mission drift—creates a barrier between the mission and those who in many ways can help advance the mission further.

Shallow

The most significant gifts an organization will ever receive are usually through: 1) the outcome of long-term relationships, established through trust and confidence in the organization's leadership; and 2) a deep commitment to the mission. In a nonprofit environment, high-context relationships often evolve among staff, board members and major donors. High-context environments are faith communities, family gatherings, the regular clientele at a neighborhood restaurant, and community softball teams. In each of these examples, the community learns how to communicate not only with words but also nonverbally.

Unfortunately, only shallow, low-context relationships can survive in an arm's-length fundraising culture. The other three restraints (cheap, quick, and low-risk) don't allow for the insights in understanding non-verbal communication. We don't have time for a lunch table conversation, asking in person risks rejection, and we would certainly have better luck with a crowd. In low-context environments, communication relies only on what can be written or expressed to large, broad audiences.

Shallow relationships are a key indicator of arm's-length fundraising. They mirror the relationships elsewhere in life that require contracts and adherence to rules and regulations.

Low-context environments are generally public places where we feel like strangers. These environments assume self-interest, skepticism and doubt. In such an environment, we are unable to share values and convictions that can inspire the most significant commitments.

I never met Olive Cooke. However, I have met many donors just like her. In college, I rented an attic apartment from a generous man who was notorious for his willingness to support community projects. I never saw the table top in his dining room table because it was always overwhelmed with direct mail appeals. Ironically, I don't recall many visitors meeting with him in the living room. I once visited a woman in Boston who welcomed me into her dark study where she sat behind a desk with stacks of appeals letters to her left and right. Even as I attempted to lay the groundwork for a meaningful relationship, she tried to shuffle through letters to find the latest direct mail package from our organization.

In my first fundraising position, I was confident our organization could reap the benefits of more-meaningful gifts from among the donors we already had. By reducing the necessity for new donors, I freed up time and money that could be invested in meaningful relationships with the donors we already had.

I'll never forget a man named Mr. Walker and the way he informed my philosophy of fundraising. Mr. Walker was a WWII veteran who walked with a cane to compensate for his artificial leg. He had never given our organization extraordinary gifts. Yet I was determined not to maintain a distance between our organization and our current donors, so one afternoon I stopped in to introduce myself. We talked for an hour in his driveway. From there we developed a tradition of meeting at a local steakhouse several times a year. One year, right before the Christmas holiday, Mr. Walker stepped through the front door of our office. He had a huge grin on his face, and in his hand, was a check multiple times higher than anything he had given in the past.

Owning Our Fears

THE LESSONS TO BE LEARNED from the Olive Cooke tragedy are not reserved for those in the UK. For those of us on the other side of the Atlantic, Olive Cooke matters because US fundraising practices have shaped how fundraising is implemented around the world. Professional fundraising has been created, nurtured, and disseminated from American soil. Globally, most organizations have inherited an American doctrine of fundraising that leads to an overwhelming dependency on cheap, quick, low-risk and shallow relationships. Because of this, the events surrounding the Olive Cooke story are a critique of the entire profession.

If we assumed direct mail was the nonprofit sector's only drug of choice—and that donors like Olive Cooke were the only ones trapped in dysfunctional relationships with nonprofits— we would be wrong. Addiction doesn't play favorites. Instead, it pursues all, homing in on the most susceptible prey. Special events, grant writing, and the evolving package of Web-based techniques can easily contribute to an organization developing nearly identical dependencies.

Is it merely a coincidence that our fundraising efforts are limited to direct mail, special events, grant applications, and online campaigns that all keep us at arm's length from our donors? We insist that cheap fundraising isn't our goal. What, then, is our goal? If the constraints of cheap, quick, low-risk and shallow methods of reaching donors are not deliberate decisions, what decisions are we making—and why? The problem is that we persist in combining these same fundraising practices year after year, which would strongly suggest we're not interested in changing the way we interact with our donors.

Nonprofits entrenched in arm's-length fundraising send a signal to employees, donors, and other observers. The message is that the organization's culture is stuck in a dysfunctional use of fundraising practices that should be reserved primarily for new-donor acquisition. If addiction seems too harsh an accusation to own up to, there may be a more palatable explanation for our behavior. Somehow, arm's-length fundraising makes us feel more legitimate. In our efforts to be perceived as a viable player in the nonprofit community worthy of the support of donors, we've convinced ourselves we must look like and behave like everyone else. A culture characterized by arm's-length fundraising is simply the norm we've aspired to.

In an often-cited article, Paul DiMaggio and Walter Powell argue that organizations routinely adopt practices that are not particularly efficient, but they do it because they ensure legitimacy in the eyes of their stakeholders. This concept, known as *institutional isomorphism*, explains the tendency for organizations to become increasingly similar, without creativity and innovation.

Isomorphic behavior among nonprofits can be observed in three main areas: their dependency upon a common network of major donors, their uncertainty in how to structure operations, and their lack of clarity in goals and objectives. DiMaggio and Powell might explain that fundraising practices are passed from organization to organization through board members, executives, and fundraising professionals. Whether these inherited skills and practices have a positive effect on organizational health is a question every nonprofit leader should ask.[47]

---

47 http://faculty.babson.edu/krollag/org_site/org_theory/Scott_articles/dimag_powel.html. Accessed November 9, 2017.

What we need to examine is this: whether we own up to our own addiction to arm's-length fundraising or explain that we have adopted these behaviors from a shop down the street, the eventual outcomes are generally the same. The challenge remains. Will organizational leaders recognize the cultural behaviors they've embraced and take the necessary steps to change them?

Our fundraising culture runs much deeper than how we ask for money and reverberates from deeply held beliefs and assumptions about control, communication, money, and scarcity. The most unspoken aspects of our feelings about these elements are usually the most powerful in determining how things get accomplished.

Illusion of Control

As can be expected, nonprofit leaders become overwhelmed with daily tasks and decisions. The last place they want to discover they're not in control is in raising money. Yet it's precisely in complex matters *like money* where they're most prone to create the illusion of control. The result? A tendency to design systems and processes to maintain this sense of control rather than ensuring the use of best fundraising practices. Conversely, effective fundraisers learn the more they try to control (or manipulate) their donors, the less likely those donors are to respond in a meaningful way.

The nonprofit sector doesn't have any control issues regarding giving. That's why we exist: to give of ourselves, our time, and our resources to those in need. Our passion compels us to change the world in areas that have been overlooked or disregarded. The issue we have is with receiving. After all, we didn't start an organization, organize a board, define a mission statement as change agents only to find ourselves the needy recipients of someone else's generosity. In our determination to help others, we must become an intermediary—a bridge.

The fear of indebtedness lurks behind the gimmicks we "sell" our donors: everything from tote bags to engraving their name on a wall. It rarely occurs to us that such "naming opportunities" may be more about releasing ourselves from further obligations than they are about satisfying the ego of a large donor. So, here's the question: Is the sector's fear of mission drift more about our fear of declining a gift and less about our fear of donor encroachment?

Noam Wasserman, a Harvard Business School professor and author, points to a tension within organizations between *control* and *growth*. Many CEOs start companies not to get rich, but rather to play a central role in driving and controlling the growth of the enterprise. Yet investors also want some control over the venture. The conflict between the CEO's ability to control the venture and the company's ability to attract additional resources to fuel growth is a tricky one.[48]

It's hardly surprising that some venture capitalists use the trade-off between money and control to judge whether they should invest in founder-led companies. A few take it to the extreme, by refusing to back founders who aren't motivated mainly by money. Others invest in a start-up only when they're confident the founder has the skills to lead it in the long term. Even these firms end up replacing almost a quarter of the founder-CEOs.

Still, we may criticize nonprofit leaders when their organizations grow significantly. What we miss is that, to build their "kingdom," they've actually had to relinquish a lot of control. According to Wassermann, leaders in cash-strapped, small shops are more likely to behave like kings and queens

---

48 Wasserman, N. *Founder's Dilemmas* (Princeton University Press, Princeton NJ, 2012).

of their mini-empires than their counterparts in the big shops are. What leaders of big shops have discovered is the inverse relationship between growth and control—for the organization to grow, they can't behave like ruling emperors.

Shallow Communication

Ironically, because Olive Cooke was a working-class citizen with a modest pension, the press decided she was the victim of greedy nonprofits. In contrast, when the donor is a powerful foundation or wealthy donor, we declare the nonprofit a victim of inadequate funding. The problem is neither the donor nor the recipient. The problem is how we have defined the problem itself. The underlying problem we have largely ignored is the way we communicate and interact with each other.

George Bernard Shaw once said, "The single biggest problem in communication is the illusion that it has taken place." Many nonprofits convince themselves that meaningful communication between their organization and their donors does in fact occur, but they may only be connecting on a shallow level. Instead of facilitating genuine conversation, both sides of the conversation are speaking *at,* rather than *with,* each other. And they're doing it without cues like eye contact and body language to guide them.

Psychologist and MIT professor Edgar Schein describes this communication barrier as "the culture of tell." Even if those of us in the nonprofit sector believe we are asking (for information, advice, or donations), we are usually telling (for example, telling a donor what he should do, as well as how and when he should do it). The missing ingredients in conversations tend to be curiosity and a willingness to ask questions we don't already know the answer to. Our society is biased toward telling rather than asking, because we live in a pragmatic, problem-solving culture, where knowing things and telling others what we know is valued.[49]

Arm's-length relationships are not intended to facilitate meaningful communication and cannot be expected to result in consistent, meaningful support. In other areas of life, most of us are accustomed to these types of relationships and we don't expect them to develop into closer, long-term relationships. "In arm's-length relationships, both parties retain their independence and pursue only their own interests while attempting to benefit from the goods or services provided by the other." Neither side expects the other to invest in the relationship in any meaningful way; therefore, the trust level remains low, limiting additional investment, connection, and the development of loyalty.[50]

Our Relationship with Money

In addition to maintaining a sense of control and shallow communication, arm's-length fundraising allows us to ignore the dysfunctional relationships we often have with money as individuals and as organizations. This was the essence of Henry Ford II's regretful resignation from the Ford Foundation in 1977. His remarks imply a dismissal of the role that money and economics play in philanthropy:

> The foundation exists and thrives on the fruits of our economic system. The dividends of competitive enterprise make it all possible. A significant portion

49 Schein, E.H. *Humble Inquiry: The Gentle Art of Asking Instead of Telling* (Berrett-Koehler Publishers, San Francisco, 2013).

50 Lamb, C.W.; Hair Jr., J.F; & McDaniel, C. *Marketing* (South-Western Cengage Learning, 2009).

of all abundance created by U.S. business enables the foundation and like institutions to carry on their work. In effect, the foundation is a creature of capitalism—a statement that, I'm sure, would be shocking to many professional staff in the field of philanthropy.[51]

Money pervades every walk of life. Ford understood this, and he expected the beneficiaries of his family fortune to understand this as well. Far too many organizational leaders miss the fact that many of their benefactors identify with and admire the likes of Ford and others who have prospered because of our economic system.

Addressing how religious communities relate to money, social commentator James Emery White says parishioners only hear "give," and the message often relies on guilt to compel them to do so. This narrowly focused message leads many to believe that religious organizations are concerned only with their self-serving institutional needs. In the sector in general, we can delude ourselves into thinking that we can be successful at fundraising without acknowledging that money is a critically important part of the conversation.

Money coach Karen McCall understands the unhealthy relationships many of us develop with money. After her own journey from crisis to recovery, she founded the Financial Recovery Institute (FRI). The FRI trains and certifies mental healthcare professionals to counsel individuals and provide practical tools to help transform the individuals' relationships with money.

McCall says people with ongoing financial challenges, cyclical patterns, and recurring money dramas are generally aware their struggle entails more than merely being bad at math. While "not enough" can sometimes be a problem, it is

---

51 Ford, H. Letter to Alexander Heard, *Foundation News* (March/April 1977).

often not the primary problem. At the root of many ongoing financial troubles are unhealthy patterns related to money. And yes, even fundraising professionals can be dealing with these problems.[52]

We tend to get trapped between our individual relationships with money and the relationships our organizations have developed with money. Not only does this create tension, these potentially dysfunctional relationships are often contrary to a third factor—the relationships the organization's donors have developed with money. As I say in my seminars, "Our donors got over their money issues a long time ago." While our organizations are often grasping for the next dollar to pay yesterday's payroll, our donors have usually arrived at a much healthier place.

Three Types of Gifts

In my seminars, I begin by asking participants to identify three types of gifts they would give to an organization. Regardless of age or affluence, my experience has shown that many active donors are routinely giving all three. The first gift I ask them to identify is what we call a trivial gift. This gift may be relatively small and unsubstantial, without any intent or obligation to give again. Here's an example: Say a friend or family member invites us to support an event for a cause—like a walk or run to raise money for a certain medical condition. In this scenario, we would likely give a trivial gift.

Most of us give trivial gifts of little consequence to our personal finances. For some, a trivial gift may be equal to our monthly cell phone bill or the cost of dinner out at a nice

---

52 McCall, K. *Financial Recovery: Developing a Healthy Relationship with Money* (New World Library, Novato, CA, 2011).

restaurant. For others, these gifts may be much more—or much less—in terms of actual dollars.

Fundraising professionals routinely refer to trivial gifts as "go-away gifts," or "trust gifts" (not to be confused with a trust fund). A go-away gift implies the donor is being polite by giving, satisfying the solicitor's expectation of a gift, and yet doing so without any intention of further support. A trust gift may be a test. Will the organization use the gift in accordance with that donor's wishes, and will it acknowledge the gift in the way she expects?

Whether a gift signals "leave me alone" or represents an opportunity to earn someone's trust, the organization has some work to do if it expects more meaningful support. Talented fundraising professionals recognize the value of every gift without making assumptions about whether any single gift is an accurate indication of a donor's giving capacity. Drawing conclusions about future giving potential from a single gift is dangerous, yet common. Nonprofits are notorious for drawing a whole host of conclusions by looking at an initial, often trivial gift. The trouble is that these conclusions can be significantly off-base.

Checking our assumptions can be especially helpful for those who want to think only the best of their donor's contributions. We want to believe that our donors are contributing to our cause in the most meaningful ways. We hope the contributions they're making reflect some measure of commitment—yet rarely do we have conversations adequate for determining whether that's the case. To debunk these assumptions, I ask my seminar participants to identify a second gift.

This next gift is a *meaningful gift*. As its label implies, these gifts often have a story behind them: life-changing experiences, gratitude for an opportunity earlier in life, a strong value or conviction. The meaningful gift reflects an interest in (and a commitment to) the cause, and generally requires some planning before it is given.

Since most people don't carry cash around in significant amounts (if we carry any at all), the gift isn't given immediately. For many of us this contribution can be anywhere between a new car payment and several mortgage payments. While we may give any number of smaller gifts throughout the year, few of us can give more than three or four meaningful gifts each year. Perhaps one of the few things that trivial and meaningful gifts have in common is that they can both become a habit, typically given at the same time each year.

The third and most elusive gift is what I refer to as a significant gift. These largest contributions are beyond the reach of most organizations because the prerequisite is generally a meaningful relationship and a meaningful level of previous support. Significant gifts are often complex, multi-year commitments that can easily account for two-thirds of a households total annual giving.

What my seminar participants discover about themselves and their giving habits is revealing. Meaningful gifts are consistently five to ten times that of a trivial gift, and significant gifts are consistently ten times or more that of a meaningful gift, so I ask them to consider a few questions: How many of our current donors are regularly giving trivial gifts we (mistakenly) assume are much more meaningful? And if either can become a habit, which would we prefer to receive each year? And if our expectation is to eventually receive significant gifts, are we willing to make the necessary investments that ensure we get there?

What we're doing is looking at the kinds of contributions that represent our unique personal finances and our own circumstances. We're also considering the difference between a gift that may not mean that much and a gift that does. Identifying these gifts for ourselves reinforces the point that organizations receive trivial gifts every day, genuinely believing they are meaningful and that they will inspire the most significant levels of support.

Believing the Scarcity Lie

Author-activist Lynn Twist has spent four decades raising money and providing leadership in several global hunger initiatives. She has developed a deep understanding of money not as a trained economist or investment advisor but rather as a fundraising professional. Twist has discovered that scarcity is a lie that sustains itself through a powerful mythology demanding adherents submit to one of the following beliefs: a) there's not enough; b) more is better; and c) that's just the way it is. This "scarcity mindset" shows up in how we assess the financial capabilities of our existing donors—often we think they are unable to give more. We then resolve our unfortunate assumption by constantly pursuing new donors.[53]

If we go by the size of their mailing lists, most organizations have more than enough donors. The accumulation of donors over years (if not decades) has created opportunities to establish the kinds of relationships that lead to meaningful gifts. Our challenge is not to ensure we have enough new donors. Our challenge is neglecting to establish in a culture where more meaningful relationships can thrive and where more meaningful support can be the expectation.

Inherent in the never-ending pursuit of new donors are two assumptions. First, that the new donor will give our organizations amounts equal to (or greater than) those our current donors give. Second, that the new donor's gift will be accompanied by fewer expectations than those of our existing donors. Both bad assumptions. Rarely will new donors give more generously than existing donors. Equally rare are new donors who, as they contribute more, develop lower expectations. Unfortunately, donors who give unreservedly to our causes without any conditions don't exist.

---

53 Twist, L. *The Soul of Money: Reclaiming the Wealth of Our Inner Resources* (W.W. Norton & Company; reprinted, New York, 2006).

For their book *Scarcity*, economist Sendhil Mullainathan teamed up with behavioral scientist Eldar Shafir to explore how scarcity creates a distinct mindset for people struggling to function with less than they need. They examined how scarcity in any form, from poverty and scheduling pressures to food cravings and loneliness, forces the brain to focus on alleviating pressing shortages. This reduces the mental bandwidth available to address other needs, plan ahead, exert self-control, or solve problems. The result of perpetual scarcity can be a life fixated on agonizing trade-offs, crises, and preoccupations. These, in turn, make it hard to think clearly and reinforce self-defeating actions. (A scarcity of income has been shown to lower mental performance as much as going a night without sleep does.)[54]

Scarcity has various effects on our brains and impedes our ability to make sound decisions. The more basic the unmet need, the more serious the effects. With fundraising, the effects of scarcity may not represent life-and-death decisions, but they can cripple—or even shut down—a valuable nonprofit that is making a difference.

In fundraising, scarcity's effects are threefold. One, thinking becomes short-term and myopic (i.e., what do we need today to survive?). Two, we focus narrowly on the deficient resources; in our case, presumably *donors with dollars*. Three, our limited focus stresses the brain, which in turn reduces our ability to think more reasonably about our circumstances. We become less effective at deciding how to spend our time and resources because our lack of them diminishes our cognitive ability.

Consistent with the research, if we're honest with ourselves, whatever we lack consumes our thinking. If we don't

---

54 Mullainathan, S. and Shafir, E. *Scarcity: The New Science of Having Less and How It Defines Our Lives* (Henry Holt & Co., New York, 2013).

have enough money, we're always thinking about money. If we're busy, we're always thinking about time. If we're dieting, we're thinking about food. That's just how our brains are wired.

Like scarcity, arm's-length fundraising wreaks havoc on unsuspecting nonprofits every day. It's the effect of making the fundraising process feel cheap for both giver and receiver, driving down the value of the relationship and ultimately interfering with the organization's ability to accomplish its mission.

In 2014, Mark Astarita, then-chair of the Institute of Fundraising and the head of fundraising at the British Red Cross, made a great observation. He noted that nonprofits ask for small donations to attract more donors; in effect, they have lowered their expectations. Astarita characterized this method of fundraising as "the Primark approach." Primark, an Irish retailer owned by Associated British Foods, now sells more clothes than any other retailer in Britain. Some say Primark has contributed to a culture of disposable fashion: consumers are encouraged to buy heaps of items and quickly discard them after a few wears. Primark is now opening stores in the US to compete with the likes of Old Navy.[55]

For retailers like Primark, the company makes its money on volume; the cheaper its goods are, the more of them shoppers buy, and the quicker they come back for more. The Primark effect (on consumers) has been described as an addiction to throwaway fashion. While its appeal to value-driven customers has ensured its profitability, questions remain about its corporate responsibilities. Do customers recognize that low wage sweat shops, child labor, and a lack of environmental stewardship are why Primark goods are so cheap? Environmentalists argue that the clothing industry is one of the dirtiest on the planet.

---

55 https://www.civilsociety.co.uk/news/-primark---approach-means-charities-don-t-ask-for-enough-money--iof-chair-says.html. Accessed November 9, 2017.

Plenty of enterprises grow and thrive on volume to drive their profit margins. What about us, though? Despite our sector's best intentions, many nonprofits embrace a mindset that allows them to churn through relationships like consumers churn through clothing. In response, donors are more likely to contribute "go-away" gifts that only contribute to a dysfunctional system—and require that we eventually come begging for the same trivial response a year later. Are our donors so limited in their giving? No. Our systems are designed for less-than-meaningful relationships, and in response, we get less-than-meaningful gifts.

So, what about our donors? Would they, could they, should they give more meaningful gifts? Sure. But first the system must change.

Moving On

AFTER SEVERAL YEARS OF DELIBERATING over the Olive Cooke tragedy, some thought leaders say it's time we move on. I would say we've missed the point. Certainly, Olive's death was a tragic event that shouldn't have happened. However, the lessons to be learned run much deeper and have far greater implications than whether a tsunami of direct mail and telemarketing contributed to her death. Olive's death shone a spotlight on the outcomes of the sector's addiction to arm's-length fundraising. Were it not for her tragic death, the interrogation of our fundraising practices might have been avoided—until another incident of similar magnitude forces us to pay attention.

I've searched for a report of a fundraising professional's testimony of direct and meaningful interactions with Olive. The result? Not one single story about meeting her in her living room or even the recollection of a memorable phone call. What are the odds that a donor could be described as so generous to so many organizations for so long, and yet never have a meaningful conversation with any of them?

Look, I get it. The argument usually goes something like this. We have thousands upon thousands of donors, most of whom are giving small gifts. We can't have tea with all our Olive Cookes and expect to achieve our goals.

Maybe it's time we quit fooling ourselves into thinking that the ends justify the means. And maybe it's time we give up on the notion that no gift is too small. If we cannot afford meaningful engagement with a category of donors, then we don't continue to ask for their support. Nor do we pawn them off to another organization. By relying solely on a utilitarian approach to fundraising, we in effect create our own victims. Like the displaced and marginalized that our mission statements call us to serve, our approach to fundraising creates a category of its own.

You can be certain that, in a single meeting, anyone with six months of fundraising experience and some emotional intelligence could have learned what apparently 100 organizations never did. They could have discovered that Olive was being bombarded by solicitations every day. They could have explained to her that she was, in effect, contributing to her own misery. They could have encouraged her to consolidate her gifts to fewer organizations. Had she agreed, she might have taken the first step in ensuring that her gifts were having a measurable impact for a select few organizations.

The question of whether every meaningful interaction with a current or prospective donor requires a cost-benefit analysis is a question fundraising professionals should ask themselves very early in their careers. And it may be the most profound question that fundraisers can ask of a prospective employer to evaluate their grasp of effective fundraising. Here's the thing: the most mature fundraising operations don't expect every relationship to be a home run. Every major gift fundraiser who has successfully solicited a million dollars has also unsuccessfully asked for millions more. The best fundraisers find great joy not only in where they've discovered a sure thing, but also where they've been surprised. The most significant opportunities are often discovered in the most unsuspecting places.

Surprisingly, it's not necessarily the less affluent who get overlooked; it's simply those who the system defaults to arm's-length fundraising. I've met many Olives in my two decades of fundraising, and many of them had exponentially more capacity to give than they were assumed to have. Unfortunately, the way many organizations approach even their most affluent donors is with no greater depth or sincerity than those who were appealing to Olive Cooke. Up close and in person can be just as shallow when all you're there for is to collect a check.

Consider for a moment the three (as they are sometimes referred) true professions: medicine, law, and divinity. When a physician, attorney, or priest refers to a relationship with a patient, client, or parishioner, we all have a clear sense of what that relationship entails. In all three cases, these relationships are characterized by a twofold commitment: high-context communication and high expectations. As fundraising professionals, if our aim is for the highest levels of professionalism, then we should require of ourselves and our employers—and most important—our donors, this same twofold commitment. Fundraising professionals should be recognized for meaningful relationships with the Olive Cookes and the Bill Gateses and everyone in between. Regardless of whom they happen to be, our current donors who we intend to ask again for gifts are our first obligation. When we accept a gift, we need to recognize this has far greater implications than when we ask for one.

The war for fundraising talent will be won by those who can combine a highest standard of professionalism with an organizational culture that thrives on meaningful engagement. As we go forward, we will check our assumptions on passion and other prerequisites we might expect of fundraising professionals. We'll also consider how professional expertise evolves over time and how a mature fundraising operation evolves. Finally, we'll explore a new definition of fundraising talent and the distinct and deliberate practices that fundraising professionals can be recognized and admired for.

Harvard's Fundraiser

FIFTY YEARS AGO, FUNDRAISING WAS not a professional career path. For quite some time, those of us doing the hiring didn't understand how to characterize the ideal fundraiser, because there was no standard, no guideline, no best comparisons. The way to hire at the time was to try to match what we seemed to need with the resumes on our desks. For decades we believed a friendly, outgoing personality, combined with a passion for the cause was all we needed for successful fundraising.

During this same half-century, psychologists and economists have given us a greater understanding of who we are as individuals. We now have a better idea of how we're wired—and how we can best contribute in the workplace. Today, we better understand the passion that might compel us, the motives that might persuade us in one direction or another, and what comes with us versus what stays when we change employers. Through the lens of one celebrated, but ill-fated fundraiser, we can understand how these characteristics about ourselves might affect our organizations' fundraising outcomes.

Neil Rudenstine

Scholar Neil Rudenstine was president of Harvard from 1991 to 2001. An Oxford Rhodes Scholar, he earned a BA from Princeton and a PhD from Harvard (in English literature). Rudenstine spent twenty years at Princeton as an English professor and administrator. Not, you'll agree, the profile of someone we would expect to make fundraising history.

When Rudenstine began his tenure at Harvard, there was a $42 million deficit—another $5 million worse than the prior year. He needed to rectify this and build confidence in his leadership.

After planning for two whole years, Rudenstine launched the largest Ivy League capital campaign to date. It surpassed its goal by *a half billion dollars*. He grew the university's endowment so much it positioned Harvard as the world's second-largest nonprofit (behind only the Roman Catholic Church). However, this remarkable achievement came at a cost that overshadows his legacy as one of Harvard's greatest fundraisers.

While president there, Rudenstine created a "private time distribution formula" to keep his priorities straight. He would devote no less than half his time to the intellectual life of the institution—academic planning, faculty searches, tenured appointments—and no more than a third to fundraising. The rest of his time was to be dedicated to administrative duties.

"If I went through a week where I hardly had a chance to think about academic planning, then I would make a very powerful correction the next couple of weeks," Rudenstine explains. [56]

You needn't be a friend of Rudenstine's nor a nonprofit executive to understand what happens when people tie themselves to this kind of system. Leaders like Rudenstine experience a sense of regret over being pulled away from the mission, and yet are aware the mission obligates them to do so. The mission itself, then, becomes a double-edged sword that compels them to repeatedly carry out tasks they'd prefer not to perform.

---

56 Worth, M.J. *Leading the Campaign: Advancing Colleges and Universities*, American Council on Education Series on Higher Education (Rowman & Littlefield, Plymouth, UK, 2010).

Exhausted

In late 1994, Harvard officials announced that Rudenstine was suffering from "severe fatigue and exhaustion of unknown origin." Disappearing for three months of rest and relaxation, Rudenstine found himself on the cover of *Newsweek*, above the headline "EXHAUSTED."

The article noted, "After three years of intensive nonstop toil in a hypermetabolic climate, Rudenstine hit the wall. His life was devoured, his sleep habits scrambled, his waking minutes assaulted by a hail of never-finished tasks." Medical tests, not surprisingly, indicated his exhaustion was a result of overwork and not enough sleep. Rudenstine's condition was due in large part to the stress associated with the campaign—and his self-imposed time formula.

Rudenstine resigned in 2001, just as the university began considering another capital campaign. As he left, he expressed regret for not having had the flexibility to get to know the school better during his tenure. Despite his fundraising achievements, *The New York Times* chose to point out, ". . . [U]ndergraduates said they rarely saw him between a welcome handshake freshman year and commencement."[57]

Others criticized him for failing to take advantage of his platform as a steward of the nation's oldest and most prestigious university. The president of *The Harvard Crimson*, the university newspaper, noted Mr. Rudenstine "was clearly a brilliant fund-raiser, but to most students, that's all he was: Harvard's fund-raiser."

Rudenstine's experience at Harvard resembles what psychologists refer to as an obsessive passion—a stubborn side of passion that insists on its own way and demands

---

57 http://www.nytimes.com/2000/05/23/us/harvard-president-announces-plans-to-quit-next-year.html. Accessed November 9, 2017.

a disproportionate part of a person's life. I note here that obsessiveness doesn't necessarily get in the way of goals. However, if this is the primary passion driving people, once goals are achieved, they experience burnout.

Obsessive passion often demands that people force themselves into an identity that doesn't align with who they are. As admirable as the financial outcomes were, Rudenstine's identity was in harmony with that of a professor with his students and a renowned scholar of English literature and poetry—not that of a remarkable fundraiser. Rudenstine may have spent the first half of his career envious of a role he eventually took on only to discover it was nothing like he'd imagined.

His story reflects many fears nonprofit executives have about fundraising, beyond the fear of asking for money. Those who are determined to change the world don't want to be known as "just fundraisers," any more than they want to become the poster child for the overworked executive. They fear betraying the mission by prioritizing money over relationships. Or they fear losing control of the organization. When they assumed their senior post, they never imagined that fundraising could define their own success or failure as a leader.

Fundraising's Identity Crisis

The fundraising profession continues to contend with an identity crisis it can't shake. There are many in the field today who have spent years, if not decades, struggling with their identity as fundraising professionals. They prefer other titles and miss the opportunity to convey the importance of their task, fearing that the essence of their job description might be exposed and misunderstood. Many fundraisers have become quite good at what they do, have achieved remarkable goals, and yet have relied on a forced, obsessive passion, rather than a passion that aligns with who they are.

Like Rudenstine, fundraisers who came up through the ranks organically may have spent years struggling, like square pegs trying to force themselves into round holes. These long-tenured fundraisers continue to tussle with feeling like institutional beggars, necessary evils, or the sector's awkward stepchildren. And, like Rudenstine, they may have accomplished their task with success, but their health and quality of life have suffered along the way.

The UnderDeveloped study noted, "[F]undraising is still fighting to be recognized as a profession, even though it has many of the characteristics generally associated with professional status (a body of knowledge, a professional association, education programs, and a code of ethics, among others). Leaders from across the sector—not just those focused primarily on fundraising—should join together to promote fundraising as an attractive and rewarding career and the development director role as integral to positive change in our communities."[58]

Fundraising is not the only profession to struggle with an identity crisis. In *The Lawyers Myth*, Walter Bennett describes one that the legal profession has. While the historical (and favorable) mythology representing the lawyer was Abe Lincoln, today's lawyer is perceived to be a greedy, cynical manipulator of access and power. Bennett refers to this crisis as a self-inflicted wound "that will not heal until we begin to ask ourselves the essential mythmaking questions about who we are and whom we serve."[59]

---

58 Bell, J., Cornelius, M. *UnderDeveloped: A National Study of Challenges Facing Nonprofit Fundraising* (CompassPoint Nonprofit Services and the Evelyn and Walter Haas, Jr. Fund, San Francisco, CA, 2013).

59 Bennett, W., *The Lawyer's Myth: Reviving Ideals in the Legal Profession* (Univ. of Chicago Press, Chicago, 1943).

As a clinical law professor at the University of North Carolina, Bennett saw that, while attending law school, many students lost the confidence and self-respect that accompanied their ideals when they began their studies. They arrived to pursue a social agenda with some notion of justice at its core. Consequently, they discovered justice might not be the point; worse, it could hinder their success in the legal system!

We're all familiar with the characterization of a no-holds-barred, go-for-the-jugular trial lawyer—or an overbearing, relentless, and humorless office lawyer, one who measures success by demonstrating superiority, usually by winning. According to Bennett, these negative stereotypes are pervasive and deeply affect lawyers' professional psyche: "It has destroyed our professional mythology...our capacity to create professional myths that allow us to grow and to understand ourselves and the social and moral significance of our profession." It is exactly this type of disillusionment that I worry about in the nonprofit sector.

The Passion Predicament

Recently, I spoke to young fundraising professionals about their career aspirations. As they introduced themselves, I was hoping someone would say her decision to be a fundraiser wasn't solely based on passion for a cause. No luck. One after another, each participant espoused an affinity of some sort to make a difference in a cause.

Now, there's nothing wrong with this. But as a motivator, it won't lead to a long fundraising career. Researchers who study other professional paths have come to the same conclusions about the role passion plays—or does not play—in our careers.

Enticing "career" advice is tossed about regularly these days. "Follow your passion." "Do what you love." With empty promises like these, we've convinced ourselves and the generations behind us that pursuing the work you love is the path to career utopia.

Cal Newport, a professor at Georgetown University, developed what he calls a passion hypothesis explaining why turnover in the workplace is so high among young people today. He says the passion hypothesis has risen to the status of an absolute since Steve Jobs' commencement address at Stanford in 2005.

While Jobs' address encompassed everything from his adoption as a child to dropping out of college, and from founding multiple companies to his diagnosis with cancer, all people seemed to hear was "follow your passion." They surmised that the key to occupational happiness was to figure out what you were passionate about—and then simply find a job that matches that passion. [60]

What's evident if you read Jobs' commencement address is something else altogether. Just as Jobs did, we're more likely to *stumble* onto life passions rather than being able to *follow* them.

Miya Tokumitsu, author of *Do What You Love: And Other Lies About Success and Happiness,* warns that "Do what you love," synonymous with "follow your passion," makes exploiting employees much easier, because they can be convinced what they're really doing is fulfilling a passion—rather than earning a wage. This way of thinking easily leads to the belief that work is *not what we do for compensation*, but something that is an act of love. While "do what you love" sounds harmless, it is ultimately inward-focused, to the point of narcissism, absolving us of any obligation to acknowledge or improve the world. [61]

---

60 Newport, Cal. *So Good They Can't Ignore You: Why Skills Trump Passion in the Quest for Work You Love* (Hachette Book Group, New York, 2012).

61 http://www.slate.com/articles/technology/technology/2014/01/do_what_you_love_love_what_you_do_an_omnipresent_mantra_that_s_bad_for_work.html. Accessed November 9, 2017.

Name Your Passion

But is passion only about doing what you love? Passion can fuel motivation, enhance well-being, and provide meaning in everyday life. However, passion can also arouse negative emotions, lead to inflexible persistence, and interfere with achieving a balanced, successful life. So, is passion only good or only bad? Let's consider the two kinds of passion, *harmonious* and *obsessive*, and see how they differ.

When we freely engage in an activity because it is important to us—not because we anticipate rewards (such as potential income)—we're often embodying harmonious passion. We are generally not compelled by external pressure or obligation; we participate in the activity voluntarily. Harmonious passion can occupy a significant part of our identity, but *it doesn't create an imbalance in other areas of our lives.*

Obsessive passion, on the other hand, means we're responding to pressure to meet expectations beyond our control. It very quickly demands a disproportionate part of our identities and causes conflict with other meaningful areas of our lives. This kind of passion doesn't contribute to satisfaction with our work; instead, it raises the likelihood of burnout—or worse. Many of us are familiar with the stories of leaders whose determination to change the world has wreaked havoc in their personal and professional lives.

It's questionable whether the young professionals at the AFP gathering we talked about earlier were passionate about raising money, achieving their goals, or even building relationships with donors. They may be devoted to their nonprofit's mission. Even so, I suspect they may be relying on a forced passion to continue in their fundraising work. Harmonious passion is the kind that aligns itself with our identities and well-being without conflict. It's much more promising for staying the course. Let's face it: our sector has a passion predicament. To resolve this—

and to ensure long-term employment and commitment—we must cultivate a harmonious passion for fundraising.

First, our sector needs to raise up a new generation of fundraising professionals who don't question the legitimacy of their roles. Neither should they dismiss the contribution they make within the nonprofit and for the greater good of society.

Second, nonprofits can't rely on the demand for talent and earning potential to compel young professionals into the field of fundraising. We need to make sure both existing and up-and-coming fundraising professionals learn to be inspired by more than simply their passion for the cause. Otherwise, it's unlikely we'll be able to shake our identity crisis, reduce turnover and reach the goals required to accomplish our mission.

I have found the most talented fundraising professionals develop a complementary passion oriented toward donors who have a passion for the cause. These individuals jump out of the bed in morning to interact with individuals who want to demonstrate, through their generous support, a commitment to effective change and a confidence in those who can carry it out. I sometimes refer to this as a dual orientation to the mission; fundraising professionals are oriented toward those whose relationship with the organization is to give rather than receive.

Implicit Motives vs. Explicit Goals

When deciding among a group of candidates, it's easy to be impressed with an applicant's track record, personality, and charm. We can also be fascinated with personality assessments that explain behavior and pinpoint motivations. From these we try to predict how people might behave in certain situations or with colleagues, such as how effective they might be at developing new relationships or orchestrating the details of a campaign. One area of personality research, implicit motives, has gained prominence in recent decades but has yet to take hold in how we select fundraising candidates.[62]

We can better understand ourselves and our people by clearly distinguishing between *implicit* motives and *explicit* goals. This distinction offers a more thoughtful response to the challenges we're facing in our maturing profession. Could it be that a misalignment between the fundraisers' explicit goals and implicit motives is to blame for the high turnover in many development offices?

I've developed a typology to improve our understanding of the underlying forces we encounter every day in professional fundraising. These three personalities provide a framework for: 1) better informed hiring decisions; 2) more effective coaching; and 3) reduced turnover.

Let's start by defining implicit motives. These are preferences or tendencies toward an incentive, such as achievement, affiliation, or power; or to avoid threats, such as failure, rejection, or control by others. Most of us are unaware of the implicit motives that influence our behaviors, which are often best understood through others' observations.

Among fundraising professionals, organizations can observe implicit motives playing out through how we interact with donors, organize events, and participate in collaborative settings. They can note those of us who approach our tasks with strong determination and others who relish relationships as the centerpiece of nearly everything we do. Some of us hope our influence and reputation will afford us a sure path to greater achievements. When we're tired or

---

62 Schultheiss, O.C. & Brunstein, J.C. *Implicit Motives* (Oxford University Press, 2010).

lacking confidence, we tend to avoid situations where we might make a mistake. Or we'll hesitate for fear our requests will be denied—and then there's the possibility a major donor may have unreasonable expectations in exchange for a generous gift.

That one individual's implicit motives differ from another's doesn't surprise us. What isn't always considered is the tension between an individual's implicit motives and the same individual's explicit goals. Explicit goals represent everything we might put on paper, communicate to others, and evaluate with our boss. Rarely do we confront the fact that an explicit goal— for example, asking for money—may be at odds with an implicit motive—say, a strong tendency to fear and avoid the possibility of rejection.

In other words, we may want to achieve something for a certain internal purpose or reward, something that fulfills a need, rejuvenates us, or enhances our life. At the same time, we are tasked with certain goals and objectives for our employers. Our instincts and actions can operate independently of each other. If these aren't aligned—if they're out of sync—we run into situations like Rudenstine's. Alignment can mean we respond to stressors in ways that positively affect our health and well-being. Misalignment is just the opposite. Wired as a Renaissance literature professor, Rudenstine was expected to raise funds, something that didn't energize him or suit his internal motivation. For him, it might have felt draining, frustrating and full of inner conflict.

Here's what I've observed: A misalignment between explicitly stated goals and implicit motives is a key explanation for high turnover among fundraising professionals. Warring motives with explicit goals, such as the desire to achieve a fundraising goal yet avoid rejection, can thwart even dedicated fundraisers. Our job as a sector is to gain understanding of this conflict so we can help professional fundraisers succeed despite any unconscious ambivalence. I believe this will go far in reducing the turnover that impedes the progress of our nonprofits.

In my two decades of experience with fundraising professionals, I've encountered colleagues who tend to gravitate either toward or away from typical fundraising responsibilities. This influences how they plan, how they prioritize their time, and how they interact with donors. By understanding what drives them, we learn how their decisions can affect our fundraising culture. Despite their best intentions, fundraising professionals demonstrate patterns and habits that interfere with their effectiveness.

For example, I've always been quick to engage with major donors and solicit their support. However, if my goals included event planning and writing grants, I could always rationalize my time and attention toward those activities I was more comfortable with. As our patterns and habits begin to conflict with the expectations of our supervisors, board members, and others, it's increasingly likely we will either resign or be terminated. For example, several of my previous board members were fond of an annual golf tournament that rallied the support of our community. My eventual departure was largely a reflection of the misalignment of my job description and my preference for other areas of responsibility; namely, opportunities for meaningful engagement and the thrill of direct solicitation.

Among a long list of implicit motives, three tend to compel us the most: the need for achievement, the need for affiliation, and the need for power. Regardless of our gender, culture, or age, psychologists explain that we all have some measure of these three motivations, with one nearly always in the driver's seat. As I continue to work with organizational leaders, board members, and fundraising professionals, I've developed a sense of where each personality finds the greatest satisfaction—or the greatest frustration—in nonprofit settings. I've characterized them as *I'll Lead the Way, Let's Work Together*, and *How Am I Doing?*

The Three Personalities in a Development Office

I'll Lead the Way has a high implicit need for control or power and will be at her best when her explicit goals are aligned with this need. We understand her need as a desire to influence, control, or impress others—and to receive recognition for these behaviors. *I'll Lead the Way* is eager to break new ground, and she expects others to follow her. She is impatient and, we must note, fearful of betrayal. *I'll Lead the Way* can be counted on to develop a plan and delegate responsibilities, yet she hesitates to be in a setting where she feels out of control. Her preference for control translates into competitiveness and a zero-sum mindset. In other words, there will always be a winner and there will always be a loser. *I'll Lead the Way* is the most likely of our three colleagues to insist, abrasively, that board members must give, get, or get off.

In working with committees, we would expect *I'll Lead the Way* to be effective at organizing an agenda, handing out assignments, and keeping everyone on task. Where she may find committee work difficult is when she must follow the lead of a less-experienced (but board-appointed) volunteer chair. Of the fundraising responsibilities *I'll Lead the Way* may be the most suited for, event planning may be the place where she can truly shine. Unfortunately, she can find it difficult to be patient with a major donor as she cultivates a significant gift. She may also find it hard to envision the exchange as a win–win for both the organization and her donor.

Let's Work Together has a high implicit motivation for affiliation. Naturally, he'll rise to his highest level when his goals harmonize with this. We recognize this need as a concern with establishing, maintaining, or restoring a positive emotional relationship with another person or group. *Let's Work Together* is eager to work as a team and he expects others to enjoy collaboration as much as he does. (Of course, not everyone does.) He admits he's disorganized and fearful of rejection. *Let's Work Together* is always enthusiastic about building new relationships, but hesitates to work independently. His preference for collaboration and interaction with others will sometimes lead to an unwillingness to work autonomously and an inability to accept responsibility for outcomes.

In committee work, *Let's Work Together* enjoys the collaborative process and willingly allows board members or other volunteers to chair. If he's charged with leading the committee, he may assume too much responsibility himself and fail to delegate. Similarly, organizing a special event will be equally difficult. Fundraising may be the most difficult for *Let's Work Together* when the focus turns toward cultivating individual donors and direct solicitation. He's likely to be especially fearful of the effects a request for funds could have on his relationship with donors.

How Am I Doing? has a high implicit desire for achievement and will succeed most easily when her goals line up with this. The need for achievement is an unconscious, recurrent preference for rewarding experiences that relate to improving performance. Therefore, *How Am I Doing?* is eager to pursue reasonable goals, and she expects to receive constructive feedback. She prefers to work by herself, and what she fears most of all is failure. *How Am I Doing?* expects clear, measurable goals and would rather work independently or with peers tasked with similar goals. Her preference for independence can lead to isolation and detachment from the team.

When working on a committee, *How Am I Doing?* tends to be cooperative, eager to participate in discussions, and quick to define goals and objectives for the matter at hand. However, she can be quite ambitious and is more inclined to work on her own. That way, she can achieve her goals on her own terms.

Most of our executive directors, especially those in small shops, align with my definition of the *I'll Lead the Way* type. They have a sense of where the organization needs to go and are willing to take the lead in making sure everyone gets there. They tend to hire *Let's Work Together*—the friendly, outgoing person who likes making new friends and working as a team. The problem is that *Let's Work Together* usually hits a wall when he must ask for money because the possibility of rejection scares him away.

I've noticed small shops are the least inclined to hire and retain our friend *How Am I Doing?* We find it especially difficult to supervise this ambitious go-getter who prefers clear goals and the opportunity to work independently. She tends to step on toes and shake up the apple cart if it's getting in her way. Part of what we misunderstand is that *How Am I Doing?* isn't always after a pat on the back or a raise. She thrives on constructive feedback to help her improve her craft. In the absence of a clear measuring stick and helpful guidance, she reverts to whatever performance indicator she can find (e.g., advancement opportunities and pay increases).

So how do we search for—and recognize—the right individuals for the job? I see a lot of fundraising ads that lack an understanding of what it takes to form a lasting, mutually rewarding employment relationship. The ads seem to assume a package of skills that even the most experienced fundraising professionals can't bring with them. Identifying and attracting talent is our critical task of the hour. In the past, nonprofits have often relied on a fundraiser's past performance to gauge how well he will do in their own organization. But this isn't necessarily the case.

You Can't Take It with You

Past performance does matter, but what's important is what candidates bring with them and how well their implicit motives line up with their external goals. My experience indicates I've brought a harmonious passion for fundraising to organizations. When I'm at my best, I'm driven by the opportunity to achieve a goal. This combination, paired with my outgoing personality, has made me a good fundraising candidate and has kept me consistently employed. However, what my employers (and I) have also learned is that, regardless of my track record, I can't bring certain aspects of my past performance with me. And it's not just me.

Our value as employees consists of contributions we bring with us because of who we are—*plus* the investments employers have made in us. These are, basically, two different kinds of "human capital." *General human capital* is something that is valuable to a current employer as well as to future employers, such as formal education. *Firm-specific human capital* is usually of worth only to one employer, such as customized on-the-job training. Identifying these two types of competencies helps us analyze the value of our employees and how we can further develop them.

Relevant skills and resources that are transportable are quite valuable to prospective employees. However, several are not; they're firm-specific. Naturally, both the previous employer's management practices and its fundraising culture are left behind. But by far the most regrettable resources fundraisers leave behind are the organization's donors with whom they've developed relationships.

Here's the thing: It would take a nearly identical (or overlapping) network of donors, along with a similar fundraising culture, performance expectations and support, to predict an equivalent outcome for an individual. What are the chances of this? Not going to happen.

On occasion, I've spoken with executive directors who were leading a young organization and yet were determined to hire an experienced fundraiser. They hoped this talented professional would bring immediate outcomes and an impressive return on investment. As graciously as I can, I've done my best to explain that this may not work.

In addition to everything a fundraiser might be able to do for the new organization, he will arrive with more expectations than the organization is ready—or able—to provide. What these hopeful leaders often miss is that fundraising professionals inherit their constituencies; they don't have the privilege of creating them from the ground up. This is largely the same for the fundraising culture and their supervisors' expectations.

In situations like this, it's preferable to align the fundraiser's level of experience with the organization's current fundraising capacity. If either significantly outpaces the other in terms of experience, what you get is unmet expectations, either on the part of the fundraiser or the nonprofit. Let's say an organization has been in operation for two years. The likelihood of a robust fundraising program is not so great. Rather than hire a ten-year fundraising veteran, it's more fruitful to identify a relatively new candidate, one as determined to succeed as a fundraiser as the organization is to accomplish its mission.

A study in the late 1990s began tracking high-performing CEOs, researchers, and software developers, as well as leaders in investment banking, advertising, public relations, management consulting, and law. They discovered that top performers in all those groups were unable to sustain their successes after a job change. They were more like comets than like stars—blazing successes with their previous employers, but quickly fading out when they left to work for another company.[63]

---

63 Groysberg, B. *Chasing Stars: The Myth of Talent and the Portability of Performance* (Princeton University Press, Oxfordshire, UK, 2012).

Researchers followed the careers of 1,052 stock analysts who were ranked best in their fields. "Star" status faded quickly when switching to work for new banks. *Nearly half* of the analysts (46%) experienced waning job performance in the first year. Not surprisingly, an even larger group (65%) switched jobs within five years.[64]

Obviously, high-performing stock analysts don't suddenly become less intelligent or lose a decade of work experience overnight when they change employers. What changed was *everything the star couldn't take with her.* In addition to her personal competencies and capabilities, her high performance reflected her customers, the systems and processes of her organization at the time, its infrastructure and culture, and other resources. These all contributed to her success.

While many of us have an instinctive faith in talent, we tend to be unaware of how much an organization contributes to an employee's success. It's not likely many "stars" would change employers if they understood just how much their performance was linked with their employer. There's a secret ingredient involved that many of us fail to identify. Vital to an individual's success is an organization that gives talented employees the resources and support they need to become rock star performers.

---

64 Ibid.

A Tale of Two Ryans

MUCH OF THE INSPIRATION FOR this book has arisen from my interactions with two young men who both discovered fundraising shortly after graduating from college. Coincidentally, they are both named Ryan. Unlike Rudenstine, who aligned most of his career with a passion for the humanities, both Ryans chose very early in their careers to align themselves with professional fundraising. Rudenstine, even though Harvard's campaign was the largest in Ivy League history at the time, would likely have chosen something else as the pinnacle of his career. But it's unlikely that either Ryan will end up with similar regrets. They've developed a harmonious passion for fundraising, found confidence in their craft, and are well prepared for fundraising to define their professional careers.

Part of what strikes me about these two young men is how quickly they seem to be advancing in their professional journeys. As I write this, neither is yet thirty, yet one recently accepted a role as a major gifts officer at an Ivy League university, and the other turned down an offer from one of my clients to accept a more attractive offer that didn't require him to relocate his family. I've been intrigued by their savviness as young fundraising professionals and am eager to see where their talent will take them.

During our interactions it's been apparent that they've already become aware of how their employer can position them for success. Both Ryans have realized that their employer's philosophy of fundraising will dramatically affect whether they can achieve mastery and find meaning in their work. They have not shared the same professional path thus far, and their perspectives on fundraising have been molded by diverse experiences. Yet if they were together in a room, I'm certain they would describe the ideal employer for an aspiring fundraising professional in much the same way. As a recruiter, I've found it especially important to understand how to identify similarly talented candidates for my clients.

In his book *Outliers*, Malcolm Gladwell makes the case that, for Bill Gates, Steve Jobs, the Beatles, and All-Star Canadian hockey players, success has been much less about innate talent and more a consequence of good timing. Gladwell says many success stories are more attributable to external factors rather than the internal characteristics that we often admire. What may be different about Ryan and Ryan is the timing of their entrance into the fundraising profession, versus those like me who preceded them. Both Ryans strike me as having a very different perspective of their work and being far more knowledgeable than I was at the same point in my career.[65]

A Matter of Timing

Among numerous examples of those who have benefited from good timing, fourteen of the seventy-five richest people in human history were born within nine years of one another during the middle of the nineteenth century. These nine individuals began their professional lives during one of greatest periods of economic growth in history. They were the greatest beneficiaries of new economic growth driven by the railroads, the stock market, and industrial manufacturing. Gladwell notes

65 Gladwell, M. *Outliers: The Story of Success* (Little, Brown and Co., Hachette, New York, 2008).

that, had these individuals been born earlier, their worldviews would have been disadvantaged by the pre–Civil War paradigm. Had they been born a decade later, they would have been too young to take advantage of the opportunities in front of them. Several factors explain why Ryan and Ryan may have advantages their predecessors weren't fortunate enough to have. It's reasonable to assume they'll have distinctively different careers than those of us who have trudged through the fundraising profession's earlier years. Among the most advantageous developments may be the availability of career opportunities on a global scale, the use of technology and information, access to fundraising-specific training, and the evolution toward a fundraising-first mindset.

Both Ryans have entered the sector at a time of rapid growth that extends far beyond the boundaries of North America. The growth of the nonprofit sector around the world has resulted in a steady increase in what has always been a high-demand field of work. Regardless of whether the economy is up or down, fundraising professionals have never been without wider opportunities to consider.

Along with the growth of the sector, technology and information have dramatically increased our ability to measure and understand the effectiveness of what we do—and how we do it. It wasn't until 2006 that the Association of Fundraising Professionals and the Urban Institute established the Fundraising Effectiveness Project (FEP), which has evolved into one of the largest annual philanthropic research studies in the world. This provides the entire sector with an objective assessment of our strengths and weaknesses that is all but impossible to argue with. The FEP is just one of many examples of how technology and the use of data are helping us better evaluate our work.

Coinciding with the growth of the sector and the use of technology and information is the proliferation of academic programs aimed at preparing a new generation of world-changers. I began a graduate program in nonprofit management after being in the field for more than ten years. Now, though, many aspiring nonprofit leaders will opt into such programs immediately after college. This is quite a shift.

What is noteworthy about these programs is many of them advocate a nonprofit-first mindset. Their view is that nonprofit management studies is now its own domain. In turn, this means cutting ties with the other arenas that have historically claimed nonprofit expertise such as business administration, public administration, and social work. Likewise, we can expect an increasing number of fundraising-specific programs that are not extensions of the marketing or public relations departments.

Thus, the fundraising career path will look different from now on. For example, CASE has launched a residency program for those seeking fundraising positions within higher education. These young people will begin their careers having chosen that path first and will be guided by best practices emanating from the best fundraising institutions on the planet.[66]

What if the next phase of maturity for the fundraising profession is marked by the clarity of what fundraising professionals discover early in their careers versus what they gain over many years of experience? What if Ryan and Ryan have already learned things some of us may have missed because of the timing of their first day on the job? And what if these evolving, early-career advantages aren't limited to a specific category of shops? Globally, job opportunities around the world are driving up the demand for technology, information, and training that can fast-track a fundraiser's

66 CASE North America Fundraising Residency Program. www.case. org/Career_Central/Talent_Management/CASE_North_America_ Fundraising_Residency_Program.html. Accessed November 9, 2017.

professional career. If this is true—and I believe it is—are employers ready for a new fundraising professional who arrives on Day One with a much better understanding of how effective fundraising really works?

A Matter of Perception

Since the mid-twentieth century, those who wanted to understand how human beings develop expertise have often turned to the game of chess as a familiar lens through which to consider the accumulation and use of knowledge in other, more complex areas. Take Dutch psychologist and aspiring chess player Adriaan de Groot, who wanted to understand what distinguished grandmasters from less-talented players. He discovered that the difference was a matter of perception; the context in which they see and understand the board is very different from how others see it.

One of de Groot's observations was that talented chess players' skills were notably unimpressive in other domains. This takes us back to our Ryans. Both Ryans have demonstrated a desire to have an impressive track record as a fundraising professional who knows and understands his craft. They are decidedly fundraising professionals. Because of the changes we've discussed, the fundraising profession may be nearing a tipping point where the scales will tip towards those who deliberately choose fundraising as their initial career path versus those who migrate to the field after working in other fields. Employers will become increasingly savvy in discerning whether a candidate wants to raise money versus any number of other things that don't necessarily improve their bottom line as efficiently and effectively.

One of the advantages that Ryan and Ryan have over my own professional journey is in recognizing the defining characteristics of a mature fundraising operation. Their experience combined with the experience of others has demonstrated that the size and type of organization and the affluence of its constituency are not necessarily prerequisites for fundraising success. What enables an organization to raise money as effectively as the Eds & Meds is a commitment to meaningful engagement with fewer donors, and expecting generous and increasingly complex commitments from them.

A 2010 study of 400 US hospitals revealed a pattern of maturity in fundraising operations, with the growth indicators being efficiency, productivity and complexity. The fundraising cost ratio, which calculates the amount of money an organization spends to raise one dollar in contributions, is the indicator for efficiency. To calculate productivity, you look at the contributions raised per full-time fundraising professional, together with the average contribution per donor. Finally, representing complexity are the types of contributions and fundraising mechanisms the organization employs. The findings for these hospitals were organized into three clusters. The most mature cluster was highly efficient, highly productive, and much more experienced with complex donations. The other two clusters revealed patterns consistent with "lesser" and "least mature" operations.[67]

Within the most mature cluster, the cost of fundraising was well below industry standards, yet these organizations had the highest staff-to-donor ratio, were the least dependent on cash contributions, and were much more accustomed to soliciting multi-year pledges. By contrast, the least-mature operation had a very high cost-per-dollar ratio, were heavily dependent on cash, much less accustomed to multi-year pledges, and were the most dependent of the three clusters on corporate gifts.

Like grandmasters looking at a chess board, Ryan and Ryan's perceptions of what constitutes a mature fundraising operation

---

67 www.mhsl.uab.edu/dt/2010p/erwin.pdf. Accessed July 2017.

are very different than mine were at that place in my career. After just a few years of experience, both have already experienced mature fundraising operations that have helped them—and others like them—understand what the most mature cluster is doing differently than the other two. For Ryan and Ryan, deconstructing a mature fundraising operation is not all that complex.

In a mature fundraising operation, the ratio of staff to donor is high to allow meaningful engagement with as many donors as may desire a meaningful relationship with the organization. In return, the organization expects a meaningful commitment from these donors that extends over a period of years. By comparison, the least mature operations are characterized by nothing more than arm's-length fundraising.

In looking at the mature cluster, it achieves extraordinary efficiency not by using extremely cheap new acquisition strategies, but by instead hiring employees who confidently raise the expectation that donors not only renew but eventually commit to multi-year pledges. Everything in the mature fundraising operation is oriented towards renewal. Except for gifts received after death, all gifts offer the opportunity to be renewed. I can't emphasize this enough: Leaders of the most mature fundraising operations focus on the long-term, sustainable support of current donors. Fundraising cannot break even with initial, less-than-meaningful gifts, and it is extremely rare that the first gift will be the most significant gift a donor contributes.

If the ultimate measure of effectiveness is renewal, a nonprofit's strategy must reflect an understanding of how to accomplish this. As the most mature cluster demonstrates, the staff-to-donor ratio is highest among the three groups, which allows for a higher likelihood that donors will experience interaction and opportunities to engage with living, breathing human beings. And this is where the magic happens. Not only does important work get supported. Not only do lives get changed, medical research gets financed, or the environment is protected. But also, meaningful connections are made-- connections that not only sustain the lifeblood of nonprofits but that enhance the lives for those who give and those who receive. Every renewed gift writes another chapter in the relationship between an organization and its benefactors.

Most of us have become accustomed to routinely making small contributions with minimal expectations of what the organization will do in return; in other words, unless an additional gift is expected, our expectations are generally very low. A timely acknowledgement is all that we expect in response to our gift. In contrast, when we opt to give again, our expectations change.

Usually, first-time gifts aren't renewed because of a problem with the new acquisition strategy. No, the reason they're not renewed is because most organizations lack a commitment to renewal characterized by *meaningful engagement*. Lacking this, they continue to ask donors to contribute subsequent gifts in ways appropriate only for initial gifts. Truly, the dysfunction most detrimental to our fundraising operations is in our constant attempts to raise funds with current donors we engage with as if they were strangers.

Ryan and Ryan found out early on that the methods we use to generate initial gifts are constantly evolving. Yet the most effective strategies for renewing support remain relatively static: the necessity of a meaningful relationship, as defined by the donor, followed by a timely and thoughtful solicitation in-person. The need for this personal touch increases with every additional gift. Without being focused on renewal, Ryan and Ryan discovered it's all but impossible for them to accomplish their goals. They realize the renewal gift is the most difficult to raise from a distance. The organization simply cannot expect a donor to continue to give without the opportunity to develop a more meaningful relationship at the same time.

Sorting out the Right Signals

Both Ryans realize that new donor acquisition creates a quantity of gifts that makes everyone feel good. However, it is primarily through continued, renewed support as an outcome of meaningful relationships that effect positive change. They both learned that effective fundraising is focused on meaningful relationships. Similarly, de Groot found the best chess players relied on a narrowly focused attention that enabled them to quickly assess the board and then zero in on their greatest opportunities. This cognitive ability is also known as the "cocktail party effect"—being able to pay close attention to a single conversation while standing in a room full of people talking. Our ability to selectively focus our attention allows us to filter out the noise to focus on the signal we want to hear.

One of the greatest impediments to effective fundraising is a misinterpretation of noise as a strong signal. Arm's-length fundraising makes it extremely difficult to find a positive signal amid all the noise it generates. Instead of advancing their fundraising efforts, most organizations are just accumulating donors by the thousands while convincing themselves that is a good thing. Only when called to task to address a significant need—say, a capital campaign—does it become especially evident that the committed donors they assume they have are few and far between.

Mature fundraising organizations rely on teams of fundraisers like Ryan and Ryan to filter through masses of initial, arm's-length donations to identify prospective donors who are signaling a genuine interest in the organization and long-term interest in a meaningful relationship.

Nowhere will modern technology create more confusion and frustration than where it creates enormous amounts of noise disguised as a positive signal. There are several places in our economy where the supposed advantages of increased volume just created a mess that's hard to clean up. The goals of repeat donors, repeat users, or repeat customers have been sidelined with the rapid accumulation of new donors, new users, or new customers; which, once it's out of control only translates into confusion, distraction, and increased costs. The greatest fallout from increased volume of additional input is the effect it has on existing donors, users, and customers.

For example, the internet has made it much easier for students to apply to college, thanks to the Common Application, the nation's leading standardized online application. Now, the process of applying to nearly 700 schools is easier. But the dramatic influx of new applicants isn't necessarily making the job of admissions directors any easier. With the larger pool of applicants comes the task of identifying students who are both the most qualified and serious enough to accept an offer if one is extended. The challenges of increased volume are not limited to just the perspective of the school; students are now finding themselves smaller fish swimming in a much bigger pond.[68]

The efficiencies afforded by technology on the front end of the application process have created a mess of inefficiencies on the back end. In some cases, a school ends up with too few students, leading to budget cuts, fewer classes, and faculty layoffs. In other cases, a school obligates itself to more students than it can handle, and finds itself unable to adequately serve an overwhelming number of incoming freshmen.

In 2016, Neil Theobald, Temple University's president, was forced to resign after he fired the university's provost for an unexpected number of acceptances in the incoming freshmen class, which caused the school to exceed its financial aid budget by $22 million. At nearby Drexel University, one of the schools

---

68 Kim, A. "How the Internet Wrecked College Admissions," www.theatlantic.com/education/archive/2016/10/how-the-internet-wrecked-college-admissions/504062/, Oct. 17, 2016. Accessed November 9, 2017.

that originally pioneered the easy online application process has seen its yield rate plummet to eight percent, despite a surge of applications. Stanford University economics professor and Nobel Laureate Alvin Roth refers to the increased volume in college admissions as "congestion" that provides appealing efficiency for the beginning of the process but results in much less efficiency overall.[69]

A Perfect Match?

For those trying to clean up the mess that cheap volume creates, there is one unsuspecting place where we might find some good answers: online dating. As it turns out, most of the online dating platforms struggle with the same disadvantages that accompany volume. The standout exception is eHarmony, the leading online dating platform. This platform has discovered something important about accomplishing its goals: it must be able to clarify exactly who its ideal users are. Despite the enormous volume of inquiries it receives every day, the system is designed to distinguish between the casual dater and those who are interested in genuine, long-term relationships.

Here's how it differentiates itself: Most of eHarmony's competitors will facilitate short-term dating relationships. But eHarmony is only interested in users committed to long-term relationships and marriage. Like De Groot's finding that grandmasters rely on highly selective attention to identify the best possible moves, eHarmony does this in its efforts to identify the best possible users for its website. In addition to a notably higher price than its competitors, eHarmony requires that users complete a time-consuming questionnaire designed to ensure interest, while rejecting those who don't fit the user

69 Kim, A. "How the Internet Wrecked College Admissions."

profile it's looking for. Once the questionnaire is complete, instead of providing users with an all-access pass to search and find partners on their own, eHarmony limits users' access by providing only a limited number of compatible matches. What eHarmony has effectively done is what adherents of arm's-length fundraising always refuse to do. Instead of creating barriers to entry, they open the gates as wide as possible, and instead of raising expectations, they lower them.[70]

In one of his experiments, de Groot placed the chess pieces on the board imitating the layout of an actual game. He asked the players, from amateurs to grandmasters, to briefly glance at the board and then recall the location of each piece. As de Groot expected, the grandmasters easily reproduced the exact layout of the game; the others could hardly recall even a few positions. His initial conclusion was that memory translates into expertise.

De Groot's conclusion changed when he revised the experiment. Rather than positioning the pieces where they would occur during an actual chess game, he positioned them randomly on the board. To his surprise, the grandmasters' ability to recall where the pieces were placed disappeared. Their inability revealed something quite remarkable: the grandmasters were not skilled at memorizing individual pieces on the board. Rather, they were recognizing *meaningful patterns* they could recall from earlier experiences. De Groot's conclusion, which has since been confirmed in other studies in other fields of expertise, is that experts develop an ability to recognize meaningful patterns that allow them to more quickly sort through complexity better than their less-experienced counterparts.

70 Teran, R. "Analyzing eHarmony's Competitive Advantage," https://rogteran.co/2015/09/24/analyzing-eharmonys-competitive-advantage/. Accessed November 9, 2017.

Neuroscientist Daniel Bor explains that our consciousness has evolved as an accelerated knowledge-gathering tool. This evolution explains the brain's appetite for information and the constant search for patterns. Bor says, "The process of combining more primitive pieces of information to create something more meaningful is a crucial aspect both of learning and of the consciousness and is one of the defining features of human experience . . . . [W]hat most distinguishes us humans from the rest of the animal kingdom is our ravenous desire to find structure in the information we pick up in the world. We cannot help actively searching for patterns, any hook in the data that will aid our performance and understanding." This appetite for understanding is consistent with Ryan and Ryan's desire to understand their work in deeper and more meaningful ways.[71]

An organization that is unfamiliar with how to advance its fundraising operation bars its employees from the opportunity to achieve their goals, while interfering with long-term development of their expertise as a fundraising professional. Most small shops foster an environment conditioned upon shallow, arm's-length relationships that influence how fundraising is carried out. To see meaningful patterns, an organization must implement a plan that allows it to evolve and to be observed. If the organization relies on a single loop of activity that generates only two points of data—the date and size of a gift—it has greatly limited its ability to see and understand the meaningful patterns that reflect how effective fundraising really works.

Arm's-length fundraising limits the ability of fundraisers to recognize patterns, interfering with their ability to continue to develop skill and expertise. This is because the most talented and in-demand fundraising professionals achieve

71 https://www.brainpickings.org/2012/09/04/the-ravenous-brain-daniel-bor/ Oct. 17, 2016. Accessed November 9, 2017.

mastery in much the same way as chess grandmasters do—by identifying meaningful patterns. In the fundraiser's case, this means understanding how the organization's mission weaves through the lives of donors, inspiring the most meaningful gifts. Unlike many of their peers who work for organizations that deliberately distance themselves from their donors, Ryan and Ryan's employers have given each the opportunity to see the meaningful patterns woven into the experiences and decisions of their donors.

What Were They Thinking?

The most meaningful patterns Ryan and Ryan may be inclined to focus on are those that reflect two types of giving decisions. Consistent with the concepts behind what Daniel Kahneman calls *dual-process modes of thinking*, donors' decisions often mirror similar behaviors. In *Thinking, Fast and Slow,* Kahneman defines two modes of thinking. System 1 represents our survival instincts, operates very quickly, and relies on our ability to recall past experiences to make quick judgements, with outcomes that typically either increase immediate pleasure or avoid immediate pain. Alternatively, System 2 refers to slower and more deliberate decisions that reflect an intentional process after reviewing more information. System 2 decisions tend to be more substantial in terms of outcome and therefore warrant the investment of a more informed, methodical process.[72]

A simplistic understanding of donor behavior might suggest extremely affluent donors at one of end of the spectrum give generously and less affluent donors at the other give modest gifts. Yet the two Ryans have learned to observe a different pattern of behavior. Many donors are giving to multiple organizations with

---

72 Kahneman, D. *Thinking, Fast and Slow* (Farrar, Straus and Girous, New York, 2011).

varying degrees of commitment. And surprisingly, the difference between the smallest and largest commitments *of the same donors* can be significant. For many nonprofits, understanding a donor's decision-making process can be far more helpful than knowing how affluent a donor happens to be.

This goes back to the two systems of decision making. System 1 gifts are consistent with what's called *warm-glow giving*, a term coined by economist James Andreoni that characterizes a sort of impure altruism, having more selfish origins, such as an emotional response to an immediate need, external pressure, or sense of obligation. This type tends to consist of numerous, smaller contributions disbursed to many organizations. Ryan and Ryan would characterize these gifts as initial gifts that open the door to more meaningful engagement, in anticipation of more significant support.

System 2 gifts, on the other hand, are the outcome of more deliberate, rational decisions that don't necessarily require an immediate cash contribution when requested. The solicitor does not anticipate an immediate commitment. These types of giving decisions tend to result in larger contributions to fewer organizations.

Not surprisingly, most fundraising professionals are unaware of how their fundraising efforts reflect this understanding of how people make decisions. One fundraising consultant explains that it's no mystery that most fundraising relies on impulsive, System 1 thinking. He points out that it "appeals to survival, appeals to social standing, appeals to authority, and so on [and these] are hard-wired into human nature." He applauds direct mail for avoiding System 2 thinking, admires the use of "heated rhetoric, the emotional appeals, everything designed to provoke an immediate visceral response." [73]

---

[73] Rubush, S. "Direct mail fundraising: why the audience for your appeals is much, much bigger than you'd think" *Philanthropy Daily* (Oct. 4, 2017). www.philanthropydaily.com/rationalizing-direct-mail-why-the-audience-for-your-appeals-is-much-much-bigger-than-youd-think/. Accessed November 9, 2017.

Ryan and Ryan's reaction might be, "Sure it works, if all you want are trivial gifts. Last time we checked though, most organizations want more meaningful support that is sustainable for the long-haul." Seeing as System 1-type giving makes up 60-80 percent of many organizations' fundraising efforts, it's no wonder renewal rates are so dismal.

The sometimes blatantly ignored flaw in relying on System 1 thinking to drive our fundraising efforts is that it undermines our ability to eventually arrive at System 2 decisions. A donor who never transitions to a more deliberate and intentional decision-making process never becomes the donor a mature operation can rely on.

The best example of System 1 decisions in charitable giving is disaster giving, which is notoriously quick but fleeting. Organizations often see a dramatic spike in giving that peaks after a few days and then falls very quickly. For example, following the 2004 South Asian tsunami, donations suddenly rose six times the normal volume. Similarly, after 2005's Hurricane Katrina, donations were twenty times the normal level.

However, the impulsive nature of System 1 giving isn't limited to a natural disaster. In 2014, the ALS ice bucket challenge raised $100 million from many people who had no idea what the disease was. In 2015, GivingTuesday raised $177M for nonprofits in ninety-eight countries. The average gift was just under $108. These are remarkable outcomes, and yet they almost all reflect System 1 decisions. These donors cannot be expected to have made especially informed decisions, nor can they be expected to give a second time to the same mission in any meaningful way, if at all.

While the differences between impulsive, lesser informed and the most deliberate, more informed gifts may seem rather straightforward, researchers have discovered the patterns of behavior behind either of these gifts is much more telling. Organizations who "educate donors," in hopes of better response rates and larger gifts, can have a negative effect on donor behavior. The research shows that by incorporating an educational component to our arm's-length fundraising efforts, thereby requiring the donor to think, may have the opposite effect than we intended. Demonstrating the impact of giving and its effectiveness may, in fact, distract these donors from the warm glow they want to experience when making these System 1 types of decisions. [74]

What is evident to Ryan and Ryan—but sometimes less obvious to organizations that might like to employ them—is that donors making System 1 decisions can create barriers to success because their decisions thus preclude more meaningful gifts. It's only by transitioning donors to System 2 decisions that they can accomplish their goals. Their experience has shown this sort of paradigm shift is difficult. Yet only by doing so can organizations hope to attract and retain the type of fundraising talent their mission deserves.

The fact is we can either expect smaller, immediate gifts of our donors, ones like those they give to any number of organizations, or we can expect larger, more deliberate gifts that represent a select number of commitments to a short list. The most mature fundraising operations rely on the latter: giving based on more purposeful, deliberate decisions. Complex, multi-year commitments don't happen with System 1 decisions which, of course, goes back to my main point. These long-term, sustaining commitments rarely happen at arm's length.

Both Ryans recognize that many initial gifts are emotionally motivated, impulsive, and given without any intent to provide future support. They also recognize the value of an initial gift is to be a doorway to meaningful engagement. Through this deeper

---

74 Karlan, D. & Wood, D.H. "The effect of effectiveness: Donor response to aid effectiveness in a direct mail fundraising experiment" *Journal of Behavioral and Experimental Economics* 66 (Feb. 2017): 1-8.

connection, they can increase the donor's confidence in the organization and strengthen her commitment to the mission. Ideally, this leads to more significant, sustained support.

The question becomes this: do we want charitable giving triggered by an impulse or informed by a more deliberate process? And are we ready to make the systemic changes in our organizations and the way we conduct fundraising—and hire talent—to reap the benefits of this for both our missions and our donors?

A New Definition of Fundraising Talent

THE CHALLENGE OF OFFERING HIGH compensation for fundraisers is usually the defense from small shops when they're accused of being addicted to arm's-length fundraising. Often, executives and boards acknowledge their approach to fundraising is less than desirable. They think, "We simply can't afford the type of individual who would raise money more effectively; therefore, we must rely on the next-best alternative."

Unfortunately, many small shops would rather throw up their hands in defeat than contemplate how their logic might be flawed and, in fact, might contribute to the problem. The reality is both small shops and big shops hold to deeply ingrained assumptions about what constitutes fundraising talent and superior performance, and what is required to arrive at either of them. Small shops don't have to employ an especially talented fundraiser or be able to afford the high cost of compensation to contribute to what keeps it so high.

As we've discussed, winning the war for fundraising talent begins with aligning our identities with a harmonious passion, one that allows us to stay in the profession without eventually burning out. We've also discovered that talented fundraisers are easily assessing whether an organization's culture will give them the opportunity to find meaning and achieve mastery through their work.

However, prospective employees aren't the only ones who should learn to recognize meaningful patterns that influence our decisions. Similarly, organizational leaders can look at patterns when making hiring decisions. As in many fields of expertise in today's rapidly changing workplace, the definitions of talent are evolving. What if there were a new definition of fundraising talent and a better understanding of the path that got us there? And what if this new definition were fully embraced by small shops? If so, this could level the playing field and ensure that all organizations could accomplish their missions.

The American composer and playwright Johnathon Larson once said, "The opposite of war is not peace; it's creation." A new definition of fundraising talent will allow organizations to withdraw from the bidding war for the shrinking pool of existing talent. Instead, they will learn how to identify, train, and coach a new generation of high-capacity fundraisers.

We've talked about the growth of the profession of fundraising and how it is coming into its own. Before we look at a new definition for fundraising talent in our sector, let's consider the experiences of a clinical psychologist who, during a professional crisis, began asking many questions that are very much like those we are asking in the fundraising profession.

Dr. Tony Rousmaniere's path to becoming a psychotherapist is a familiar one. Like most of his colleagues, Rousmaniere is a people person who cares deeply about helping his clients and wants to help them navigate the difficulties in their lives. During his first year of practice, he found himself quickly bonding with his clients and felt affirmed after seeing some of his clients respond quickly and positively to therapy. He was also encouraged to discover that even those clients who were not immediately responsive settled into a pattern of improvement after several sessions.[75]

The honeymoon was over quickly when Rousmaniere discovered half of his clients were not actually improving; they were either dropping out, stalled or getting worse. Rousmaniere

---

75 Rousmaniere, T. *Deliberate Practice for Psychotherapists: A Guide to Improving Clinical Effectiveness* (Routledge, New York, 2017).

admits that his initial reaction to his first few dropouts was outright denial. He later learned that his experiences were quite common; research suggests that forty to sixty percent of clients do not benefit from therapy. Discouraged and unaware that his batting average was typical, Rousmaniere consulted the two most likely places that could improve his professional performance: supervision and treatment methods.

Rousmaniere's first hope for improvement was the assistance of a supervisor. His supervisor was smart, friendly, and approachable, with more than three decades of experience. The two of them spent an hour together each week discussing his caseload. His supervisor provided advice, new and different perspectives on his cases, and assigned readings. Unfortunately, despite his supervisor's best efforts and strict adherence to instructions, Rousmaniere's performance was not improving. The supervision may have improved Rousmaniere's knowledge of psychotherapy; however, it proved ineffective at helping him become a better therapist.

Frustrated with the ineffectiveness of supervision, Rousmaniere also began to question the effectiveness of the methods he was using. He quickly discovered that every method of psychotherapy was supported by a handful of studies that supposedly affirmed their superiority in comparison with others. He found that, despite their distinct advantages, what all major treatment methods have in common is an unacceptably high rate of non-responders, dropouts, and deterioration. He also discovered the decision-making process that influences the choice of treatment method was more like choosing a religion rather than a scientific process based on empirical data. Rousmaniere found that most therapists choose a method based on two criteria: first, their network of professors, mentors, and peers; and second, their sense of congruence with the model. This process results in a feel-good method that isn't tethered to reality, hidden behind a veneer of scientific credibility.

Rousmaniere reached a crisis when one of his clients died after a drug overdose that resulted in her son being placed in foster care. For Rousmaniere, this was his breaking point. Aware that supervision and switching his approach were not going to ensure he could help his most desperate clients, Rousmaniere ventured outside the boundaries of his profession *and into the science of expertise.*

All professions have high hopes for the effectiveness of their supervisors and the methods that define their tasks. We also have an enduring faith in natural talent, years of experience, and the accumulation of knowledge. While Rousmaniere found himself questioning the effectiveness of his supervisors and his approach, he was also confronting the hard truth that his own natural abilities, his years of experience, and the volumes on his bookshelves weren't necessarily going to improve his patient outcomes.

Talented fundraising professionals tend to reach a similar reality check early in their careers—usually sometime between the interview and their first performance review. A charming, outgoing personality, matched with a solid track record, and regular attendance at seminars and conferences might result in an impressive job offer. But they can't guarantee measurable outcomes, and certainly not by the first performance evaluation.

After observing someone's display of remarkable talent, we've all said, "She's a natural." We conclude that this individual was born with the innate ability to be a star athlete, a brilliant physician, an extraordinary teacher. In rare moments of glory, we may have even afforded ourselves the same praise. And so it was for Rousmaniere. There were times, before he recognized the painful reality that half his clients weren't making progress, that he believed he was a natural therapist.

The notion of natural talent is widely accepted to have originated with nineteenth-century anthropologist and explorer Francis Galton. As the founding father of eugenics and the author of *Hereditary Genius*, Galton was an esteemed leading scientist of his day. Famed for coining the phrase "nature versus nurture," Galton theorized that nature determined not only an individual's physical but also his mental and moral characteristics. Galton's beliefs as to how people attain high levels of performance were compelling and continue to affect our culture's view of ability and expertise.[76]

In our contemporary era, Swedish psychologist Anders Ericsson is a global authority in expertise. As someone who has spent three decades studying the path to superior performance, Ericsson explains that our belief in natural talent comes from observing supposed natural prodigies, those who seem to exhibit extraordinary abilities with little or no training. He has spent a lifetime investigating the stories of such people. He reports with confidence that he has never found a convincing case of anyone developing these exceptional abilities without intense, extended practice.[77]

Just as natural talent is not a predictor of supreme excellence, neither are our many years of experience. Ericsson's research demonstrated that, while most professionals reach a stable, average level of performance and then remain there throughout their careers, only those who choose intentional, focused methods of improvement will reach the highest levels of professional mastery. To be clear, experience does matter; however, it will not invariably lead to expert levels of performance. What matters is the type of experience and whether that experience has been ingrained by years of what Ericsson termed *deliberate practice*; an intense focus on skill development with the sole purpose of improving performance.

---

76 www.biography.com/people/francis-galton-9305647. Accessed November 9, 2017.

77 Ericsson, K.A. & Pool, R. *Peak: Secrets from the New Science of Expertise* (Houghton Mifflin Harcourt, New York, 2017).

A large body of research has made it clear that deliberate practice is not just *important*, but is *necessary* for achieving expert performance.

Fundraising thought-leaders have made similar observations; that years of experience and accumulated knowledge may carry an unwarranted weight in recruiting fundraising professionals. Managers doing the hiring are often confronted with the challenging choice of whether to recruit from the small pool of individuals with years of experience or choose less-experienced individuals who can demonstrate key competencies and transferable skills. It has been argued that we may be able to resolve our talent shortage by recruiting individuals with little or no previous fundraising experience and provide them with the training they'll need to be successful. As Ericcson said, many nonprofit leaders have observed experience to be a weak predictor of superior performance, and only those with the tenacity, ambition, and determination to move beyond their comfort zones can achieve the highest levels of performance.[78]

Ericsson explains that the traditional approach to training and development often focuses on knowledge at the expense of skills. He believes the main reasons for this are tradition and convenience; I would add that efficiency plays a big role as well. It is easier and cheaper to present knowledge to a large group of people than it is to create conditions where individuals can develop skills. In this way, our approach to training fundraising professionals quickly begins to resemble everything else that characterizes arm's-length fundraising.

Like most professions, fundraising has an abundance of resources for improving our knowledge of our work. There

---

78 Smith, Z.A. "Assessing Educational Fundraisers for Competence and Fit Rather than Experience: A Challenge to Conventional Hiring Practices," *International Journal of Educational Advancement* 10, no. 2 (Sep 2010).

is no shortage of books, periodicals, and online resources, along with seminars and conferences designed to increase our knowledge base. We flock in droves to learn more about donor personalities, methods of giving, and gift-planning vehicles. Unfortunately, where our profession suffers from a dearth of opportunities is in skill development, which interferes the most with meeting our goals. Where the accumulation of knowledge misses the mark is in its inability to facilitate deliberate practice.

Deliberate practice is often described as the challenging, sometimes painful process of intentionally pushing ourselves beyond our current levels of performance. This deliberate practice regimen is designed to create a disequilibrium that allows professionals to break old habits and replace them with more effective ones. Ericsson distinguishes deliberate practice from other sorts of purposeful practices in two important ways, both of which are consequential to fundraising and to small shops in particular.

First, deliberate practice assumes a field of expertise that is already well-developed which is to say that the best performers have attained a level of performance that clearly sets them apart from people who are just entering the field.

Admittedly, the fundraising profession is still a maturing profession that is only now beginning to recognize who among us are our best performers. For example, a recent study of more than 1,200 major gift officers at eighty-nine colleges and universities in North America and the United Kingdom identified the characteristics of what the researchers called "Curious Chameleons." The study found that inquisitive, highly adaptable and assertive professionals represented just 3.8% of the survey population, but had 78% higher odds of exceeding goals.[79]

---

79 O'Neil, M. www.philanthropy.com/article/Curious-Chameleons-Make/152575 (Sep 24, 2014).

In addition to being able to identify a distinct category of top performers, deliberate practice also requires an experienced coach who can design a practice regimen, observe, and provide feedback.

This is an area where Rousmaniere found his profession was particularly weak. Lack of accurate feedback has been cited as one of the fundamental problems underlying an overall lack of expertise in his field. He described therapists as cloistered in isolation and secrecy, going decades without access to any expert feedback on their mistakes and failures. Many who have experience fundraising in a small shop would characterize their experiences the same way. The lack of adequate feedback from an informed supervisor or coach is certainly one the greatest weaknesses in small shops.

The following, adapted from Anders Ericsson's *Peak*, outlines the principles of deliberate practice:

1. It develops skills that have already been identified and for which effective training techniques have been established. The practice regimen should be designed by and overseen by a coach familiar with the abilities of expert performers and with how to best develop these abilities.
2. It takes place outside one's comfort zone and requires one to constantly attempt tasks just beyond one's current abilities.
3. It involves well-defined, specific goals and often includes improving a specific aspect of the target performance rather than a vague overall improvement. Once an overall goal has been set, the coach will develop a plan for making a series of small changes that will add up to the desired larger change.

4. It is deliberate; that is, it requires a person's full attention and conscious actions. It isn't enough to simply follow a coach's directions.
5. It involves feedback and modification of efforts in response to that feedback. Early in the training process, much of the feedback will come from the coach, who monitors progress, points out problems, and offers ways to address them. With time and experience, participants must learn to monitor themselves, spot mistakes, and adjust accordingly.
6. It both produces and depends on effective mental representations (hypothetical scenarios that represent external realities). As one's performance improves, the "pictures inside our head" become more detailed and effective, in turn making it possible to improve even more.
7. It nearly always involves building or modifying previously acquired skills by focusing on aspects of those skills and working to improve them specifically.

Combining Forces

Today's fundraising is markedly more complex than it was a half-century ago, when the profession was in its infancy. In working with clients with varying degrees of experience yet equally determined to get fundraising right and achieve their goals, we found something interesting. By combining deliberate practice with the wisdom of a simple checklist, organizations can overcome much of the complexity of fundraising and gain the advantages that usually come only with decades of experience. This strategic combination effectively compensates for the experience a young and aspiring fundraiser may be lacking.

In his book, *The Checklist Manifesto*, Atul Gawande says modern society generally explains failure in two ways. The first is due to ignorance of how to accomplish something, thus we fail in our attempts to gain the knowledge we lack. The second—often the more prevalent explanation for failure in professional domains—is ineptitude; we have the knowledge, but fail to apply it correctly.

Gawande tells the story of the 1935 flight competition when airplane manufacturers were vying for the opportunity to build the US Army's new long-range bomber. Boeing's Model 299 was presumed to be the winner even before the competition. Unfortunately, after a successful takeoff, the impressive plane stalled at 300 feet, crashed, and killed the pilot and another member of the crew.

The investigation revealed the crash to be pilot error rather than a result of mechanical failure. Due to the complexity of the new plane, and despite being well trained and experienced, the expert pilot neglected to release a new locking mechanism. As you might expect, Boeing lost the competition and nearly went bankrupt. The newspapers described Boeing's 299 as too much airplane for one person to fly.

Fortunately, the Army didn't completely give up on the 299 and continued to test its use. However, instead of providing more training to its already experienced pilots, the army created a pilot pre-flight checklist. Renamed the B-17, the "Flying Fortress" became a powerful force in WWII. Regardless of their level of experience, pilots today still rely on a simple, precise checklist to ensure that no critical steps are overlooked. Similar procedures have been developed for professionals in healthcare, law, transportation, and architecture—all fields where getting the task done right is essential and often where lives can be at risk.[80]

---

80 Gawande, A. *The Checklist Manifesto: How to Get Things Right* (Metropolitan Books, Henry Holt & Company, 2009).

The value of a checklist is often what *doesn't* get overlooked. One of the disadvantages of many years of experience can be a naïve confidence that occasionally clouds our judgment. In our rush to add yet another success story to our resume, we neglect the important steps that contributed to our earlier achievements.

In small shops, the advantages of experience can quickly become the fundraisers' greater obstacle to success. As is often the case, they arrive with years more experience than their supervisors and are left to chart their own course and discern the best use of their time and resources. It is often in these scenarios, where the employer assumes experience translates into an immediate advantage, that we discover even the most talented fundraisers tend to revert to the bad habits of arm's-length fundraising. This is where the combined forces of accountability to a checklist and deliberate practice regime become especially helpful. In effect, they develop the inexperienced supervisors' skills by directing their attention to key measurable indicators that lead to the greatest outcomes.

In the first half of this book, we looked at how low expectations and shallow relationships have made it all but impossible for some organizations to achieve their goals. Decades of arm's-length fundraising have destroyed many chances for them to bring about real change in their communities. The combination of a checklist and a deliberate practice regimen may be some organizations' last hope of ensuring they can sustain relationships with their most committed, most confident, most capable donors before it's too late. This combination by no means represents a comprehensive fundraising strategy. Rather, it offers an opportunity to ensure the organization's understanding of how effective fundraising really works.

For our clients, aligning their understanding of how effective fundraising works begins with a deliberate practice regime, one that reflects a commitment to a higher staff-to-donor ratio, meaningful relationships in anticipation of meaningful support, and direct solicitation rather than asking at an arm's length. In accordance with this commitment, our checklist consists of an assigned list of donors; scheduling two weeks in advance; ensuring meaningful conversations; coordinating subsequent meetings in teams; and always asking in person, then reiterating on paper.

The Assigned List

If we were to ask most fundraising professionals what primary advantage big shops have over smaller ones, many would assume it's the size and affluence of their constituencies. This suggests that large numbers of especially wealthy people on an organization's list are the key drivers behind successful fundraising. This is only half true. The advantage behind a larger and presumably wealthier donor base is not the opportunity to engage with more people. In fact, it's exactly the opposite. The advantage larger nonprofit institutions have is their ability to segment smaller categories of donors with whom they develop long-term, meaningful relationships in anticipation of meaningful support.

The assigned list is never a random group of names a fundraiser selects but is a segmented group of donors that is assigned by a supervisor. The fundraiser spends his time interacting with each individual, establishing and cultivating meaningful relationships that eventually lead to meaningful gifts. For most organizations, the assigned list is no more than 150 donors. This is not an arbitrary number, but acknowledges our individual human capabilities.

The number 150 (known as Dunbar's Number) is generally accepted as the limit on the number of quality relationships a human being can have. This suggests a cognitive limit on the human brain for maintaining stable social relationships. The number was generated through a study of contemporary business practices, tribal societies, even relationship patterns on Facebook; repeatedly, human beings successfully organize around, at most, this number.[81]

The more active donors an organization attempts to have—and the fewer fundraising professionals they employ—the higher the likelihood of an addiction to arm's-length fundraising. At best, an organization can assume the capacity to cultivate and steward 150 meaningful relationships per full-time employee dedicating her time to an assigned list. As was pointed out earlier, the most mature fundraising operations, and those raising the most significant gifts, have the highest staff-to-donor ratios.

In addition to a nonprofit's assigned list for one fundraising professional consisting of 150 donors, we encourage our clients to fix the list for ninety days. Rather than allowing the fundraising professional the option of occasionally revising the list if she wishes, the supervisor only assists with "refreshing" the list once a quarter.

The purpose of a fixed, assigned list is twofold. First, it allows the fundraiser to give every donor on the list adequate attention. Especially at the outset, establishing the relationship may require strategic thinking and creativity. As a major donor once put it, a successful fundraiser needs a balance of patience and persistence. Second, it guards against the latest new opportunity that often distracts fundraisers from a deliberate focus on the donors the organization already has.

---

81 Dunbar, R. *How Many Friends Does One Person Need? Dunbar's Number and Other Evolutionary Quirks* (Faber and Faber, U.K, 2010).

Two Weeks Out

Jerald Panas, author of several must-read books and possibly the most influential fundraising consultant on the planet, estimates 85 percent of a fundraiser's job is getting the meeting scheduled with their prospective or current donor. If there is anything that interferes with an organization's ability to be in sync with its donors, it is the tyranny of the urgent that plagues so many small shops. As we noted earlier, some organizational leaders find it nearly impossible to free themselves from putting out fires, even though it would ensure fewer fires got started in the first place. A culture driven in this way has cost many organizations the meaningful support their missions require.

The best way to eliminate this dysfunctional habit is to create a new one—that of scheduling meetings with donors at least two weeks in advance. In other words, if we're speaking with a donor on Monday, March 1, the meeting should be scheduled for a date no sooner than Monday, March 15. The advantages of this simple, deliberate practice are quite remarkable once the new habit has taken hold.

What we often neglect to consider is that our scheduling habits send several important signals to donors. It acknowledges they are busy people and respects their schedules. It also implies we want our organization to be a priority in their schedule; we don't want to simply drop by for a few minutes. Finally, it communicates that our time is as valuable as theirs is. This is one of the first indications of a meaningful relationship. When neither party will prioritize the relationship, we cannot expect meaningful support to follow.

Initially, scheduling two weeks ahead can be a difficult habit to develop and even seems dishonest when the opportunity for an earlier meeting is welcomed. If a donor indicates that he is available in a few days, we feel inclined to accept the meeting; it's difficult to imply we're not available. Unfortunately, what this uncomfortable moment reveals is that we're not busy—and maybe we should be. If we allow the two-week window approach to stick, we will find this uncomfortable situation to become less common.

The greatest advantage that scheduling two weeks out affords the fundraising professional is the opportunity to do her homework. Rather than walk into a meeting unprepared, scheduling in advance allows for a strategic conversation with the executive director or board member who may know the donor. It may give her an opportunity to consult with colleagues about a program that may be of interest to the donor. Most importantly, it allows time for other organizational leaders to consider joining the meeting.

Meaningful Conversations

The third deliberate practice is ensuring that we're having meaningful conversations with our donors. These more in-depth conversations are opportunities for fundraising professionals to demonstrate that an organization is committed to genuine relationships with its donors. Every meeting should offer an opportunity for a meaningful conversation, and in time, fundraising professionals learn what exactly constitutes such a conversation. For those just get starting, we provide a series of questions as guidelines for the initial meetings.

These introductory conversations are orchestrated around five open-ended questions, sometimes presented in advance of the meeting, intended to create a pathway for more meaningful engagement in the future. The questions align with five key words: vision, expectations, confidence, support, and one-thing. We encourage our partner organizations to craft their own unique questions while remaining consistent with the key-word framework.

For example, the five questions might be:

1. What is your <u>vision</u> for our organization in the next five to ten years?
2. How is our organization meeting or not meeting your <u>expectations</u>?
3. How would you describe your <u>confidence</u> in our board, our CEO, and our strategic plan?
4. In addition to your support of our organization, what other organizations do you regularly <u>support</u>?
5. Is there <u>one-thing</u> you would also like us to be aware of?

The five questions are not nearly as important as the message that is conveyed to the donor. Rather than approach him as if he were unfamiliar with the organization's mission, the fundraising professional assumes that the donor is adequately informed and may in fact offer a new insight or perspective.

If charitable giving has not already become a part of the conversation, the fourth question invites the donor to share how he makes his charitable gift decisions, and which organizations are priorities. This important place in the discussion is not intended as the precursor to a solicitation. The primary purpose for this question is to acknowledge that the exchange of a charitable gift is part of the relationship and to allow money to be a part of that relationship.

Most of our clients have asked the five questions somewhat differently yet kept to the same framework for one primary reason. By relying on the same five key words, everyone at the nonprofit engaged in donor cultivation is asking the same questions and listening for consistent themes in the responses. This allows each initial conversation to contribute to a continuous stream of feedback gathered at the same critical moment in the relationship-building process.

Subs in Teams

Our fourth deliberate practice is a commitment to subsequent meetings held in teams.

This practice helps address one of the most common challenges in small shops: that of the fundraising professional feeling isolated and misunderstood. Exacerbating this, other staff of the nonprofit are uncertain and somewhat suspicious of the fundraising professional's activities. Every meeting with a donor doesn't necessitate bringing along another person from the nonprofit, but we strongly encourage our clients to commit to team visits for follow-ups, solicitations, etc. This allows the fundraising professional to establish the relationship with the donor while ensuring that other organizational leaders become engaged in the process.

Where fundraisers and other nonprofit employees often disconnect is in their understanding of each other's work and how they contribute to the mission. By prioritizing team meetings with donors, the organization creates space for consistent interaction between both categories of employees, facilitating greater understanding of each other's contributions and enhancing the quality of the donors' relationships with the organization.

The value of subsequent meetings in teams is not only for internal purposes. Donors are typically more than happy to meet with fundraisers and appreciate that there is a representative designated to them. However, these engagements can be greatly enhanced by including other members of the organizations who speak about the program and offer unique and interesting perspectives of the mission that the fundraiser traditionally cannot.

Ask In-Person, Reiterate on Paper

Our final deliberate practice is ensuring all solicitations of those on the assigned list are first done in person and immediately reiterated on paper.

In *The Art of Asking*, Amanda Palmer says her many odd jobs taught her much about the feelings of vulnerability that accompany asking and observes nearly every important human encounter comes down to asking. "Asking is, in itself," she observes, "the fundamental building block of any relationship."

As a street performer dressed as an Eight-Foot Bride, Palmer watched people approach. As they contributed money, she handed them a flower and made intentional eye contact. Palmer describes these meaningful encounters as ones with people who seemed like they hadn't talked to anyone in weeks. Without saying a word, she would communicate nonverbally, "Thank you. I see you." She would see a message in their eyes in response: "Nobody ever sees me. Thank you."

Palmer learned from her brief but profound encounters that what people desire is meaningful connection. This is the same type of connection our donors are looking for when they respond to our appeals: they're hoping for a meaningful response in return. As fundraising professionals, we are at our best when we return the favor—when we ask in person, in anticipation of, and in sincere gratitude for, a meaningful response.[82]

It is in these soliciting moments that fundraising professionals can fulfill one of our primary obligations to donors. When we ask directly, specifically and in person, donors are invited to look us in the eye and say yes, no, or maybe. When timely and appropriate,

---

82 Palmer, A. *The Art of Asking: How I Learned to Stop Worrying and Let People Help* (Grand Central Publishing/Hachette, New York/Boston, 2014).

we can be assured that our donors rarely desire to say anything other than yes. What's most important in this moment is that we allow our donors the time and place to be generous and to find meaning in their contribution. When we selfishly insist on an arm's-length exchange, we have no appreciation for this potentially powerful and rewarding moment.

In our own work as a firm, clients routinely ask us for a script. They want to role-play the solicitation. We give them the same answer we'll give you now: that's not how it works. Our clients are grasping for control or believing that adhering to an outline will eliminate their feelings of vulnerability. It won't. Palmer writes: "[A]sking can be learned, studied, perfected. The masters of asking, like the masters of painting and music, know that the field of asking is fundamentally improvisational."

When we ask in person, we ask specifically, and we ask in accordance with the organization's operating budget, strategic plan, or case for support. Rather than wait for the donor to discover an opportunity that interests her, the fundraising professional should know the needs of the organization well and be able to point to places that might align with her interest.

I once solicited a million-dollar gift only to have the donor call me a few days later to clarify what I had asked for and what he had agreed to give. We can be certain I was clear about the request I was making, and yet somehow, he missed something. In a moment like that, articulation and clarity are critical. The most deliberate practice for a fundraising professional is asking in person, with the request so precise that he can once again articulate the request on paper.

Our checklist combined with deliberate practices provides a lens through which we can envision a new definition of fundraising talent and enables fundraisers to ensure they're developing the skills that are most desirable and in-demand for their employers. It's not about competing with the capabilities of volunteers, outsourcing, and continuously improving technology; this definition of fundraising talent favors the individual who wants to be recognized and admired for what he can do better than anyone else.

Historically, fundraising professionals have been able to specialize as master technicians anywhere along the fundraising continuum that made the most sense at the time. I would venture to say this will no longer be the case. New acquisition and other highly technical, logistical, process-oriented tasks have always operated like a machine, and nonprofits, like everyone else, will continue to ensure that the process runs as efficiently as possible. With efficiency as the focus, this will inevitably cost jobs.

This is not to suggest that new donor acquisition is no longer necessary. Quite the contrary. We will always need to acquire new donors. The question we must answer for ourselves is whether organizations will continue to pay full-time employees to accomplish the earliest steps in the fundraising process. Organizations are likely to find more efficient ways to accomplish everything that comes *before* the process of cultivating a meaningful relationship.

Conclusion

'M A FATHER OF FOUR children. If there's anything Erika and I have learned as parents, it's that if we expect our children's behavior to change, then we must change our behavior first. Anyone raising children knows exactly what I'm talking about. The same can be said for fundraising and the expectations we have for our donors. To raise the expectations of donor behavior, we must first change our own.

The behavior most nonprofits must change is how we interact with our donors—most importantly, with those whose support we expect to renew. We should never again be accused of exploiting the likes of Olive Cooke for whatever value she might provide, in exchange for the shallowest relationship we can provide her in return. We need not exaggerate the complexity of having tea. Let's not let that get in the way of developing a meaningful relationship—and asking for a meaningful level of support.

If the focus of our fundraising efforts is to increase the volume of addresses in our databases while holding to the same quality of relationship and expectations of commitment they represent, we're fighting a losing battle. The nonprofit sector's dependency on arm's-length fundraising has run its course. For too long, we believed fundraising could be done efficiently regardless of its effectiveness, without the expectation of a meaningful relationship as part of the exchange. This is no longer the case. The costs have gotten too high, the competition too great, and the distractions too many.

If those who are expected to raise significant amounts of money spend most of their time and resources organizing events, mailing and emailing, and tinkering with online platforms, they undermine the opportunity to achieve their goals, master the skills that are most desirable to their employer, and ultimately interfere with the organization's ability to accomplish its mission.

If there is anything that my two decades of fundraising in the nonprofit sector has taught me, it is that generous donors and talented fundraisers generally expect the same thing. They want to be recognized and admired for the unique and meaningful contributions that they make towards mission accomplishment. The War for Fundraising Talent is already being won by those organizations that understand this similarity in expectations.

The War for Fundraising Talent *will not be won* by organizations that continue to mistake their scarcest resource as *donors with dollars*. After years of obsessively accumulating new donors, most organizations have more than enough donors to keep them busy for quite some time.

The War for Fundraising Talent *will be won* by organizations that can identify, train, and retain a new generation of fundraising talent characterized by higher expectations of themselves and their donors. Once the initial gift has been received, it will be the fundraiser's responsibility to discern who will be asked to give again. In asking for donors' renewed support, we are committing ourselves to a meaningful relationship with them, and we are expecting a meaningful commitment in return. It will be our distinct and deliberate practices, those that begin with a meaningful relationship and lead to meaningful support, that the fundraising profession can be recognized and admired for.

The Austrian psychiatrist, author, and Holocaust survivor Victor Frankl believed that man's search for meaning was his primary motivational force. Frankl explained that being human always points us toward someone or something other than ourselves. He recognized that the more we give of ourselves, the more human we become.

Similarly, German poet and philosopher Goethe wrote:

Let man be noble,
Generous and good;
For that alone
Distinguishes him
From all the living
Beings we know.

Fundraising affords citizens of our modern society an opportunity to experience two of the few things that make us uniquely human. To give and to receive are distinct human experiences. It is our responsibility as fundraising professionals, and those who employ them, to ensure that generosity and gratitude are meaningful opportunities expressed and experienced to the fullest.

Recommended Reading

Alexander, Bruce. *The Globalization of Addiction: A Study in Poverty of the Spirit.* New York: Oxford University Press, 2008

Bennett, Walter. The Lawyer's Myth: Reviving Ideals in the Legal Profession. Chicago: University of Chicago Press, 2001

Cappelli, Peter. *The New Deal at Work.* Boston: Harvard Business School Press, 1999.

Dunbar, Robin. *How Many Friends Does One Person Need? Dunbar's Number and Other Evolutionary Quirks.* London: Faber and Faber, 2010.

Ericsson, Anders and Robert Pool. *Peak: Secrets from the New Science of Expertise.* New York: Mariner, 2016.

Frankl, Viktor E. *Man's Search for Meaning.* Boston: Beacon Press, 1959.

Gladwell, Malcolm. *Outliers: The Story of Success.* New York: Little, Brown and Co., 2008

Gawande, Atul. *The Checklist Manifesto: How to Get Things Right.* New York: Metropolitan Books, 2009

Groysberg, Boris. *Chasing Stars: The Myth of Talent and the Portability of Performance.* Oxfordshire, UK: Princeton University Press, 2012

Hari, Johann. *Chasing the Scream: The First and Last Days of the War on Drugs.* New York: Bloomsbury Publishing, 2015.

Kahneman, Daniel. *Thinking, Fast and Slow.* New York: Farrar, Straus and Giroux, 2011.

McCall, Karen. *Financial Recovery: Developing a Healthy Relationship with Money.* Novato, California: New World Library, 2011.

Michaels, Ed, Helen Handfield-Jones and Beth Axelrod. *The War for Talent.* Boston: Harvard Business School Press, 2001.

Mullainathan, Sendhil and Eldar Shafir. *Scarcity: The New Science of Having Less and How It Defines Our Lives.* New York: Henry Holt & Co., 2013

Newport, Cal. *So Good They Can't Ignore You: Why Skills Trump Passion in the Quest for Work You Love.* New York: Hachette Book Group, 2012

Pallotta, Dan. Uncharitable: How Restraints on Nonprofits Undermine Their Potential. Medford, Massachusetts: Tufts University Press, 2010.

Palmer, Amanda. *The Art of Asking.* New York: Grand Central Publishing, 2014.

Phillips, Robert. *Trust Me, PR Is Dead.* London: Random House UK, 2015.

Rousmaniere, Tony. *Deliberate Practice for Psychotherapists.* New York: Routledge, 2017.

Schein, Edgar H. *Humble Inquiry: The Gentle Art of Asking Instead of Telling.* San Francisco: Berrett-Koehler Publishers, 2013.

Schultheiss, Oliver and Joachim C. Brunstein, eds. *Implicit Motives.* New York: Oxford University Press, 2010.

Slater, Lauren. *Opening Skinner's Box: Great Psychology Experiments of the Twentieth Century.* New York: W.W. Norton and Company, 2004

Tulgan, Bruce. *Winning the Talent Wars.* New York: W.W Norton and Company, 2001.

Twist, Lynne. *The Soul of Money: Reclaiming the Wealth of Our Inner Resources.* New York: W.W. Norton and Company, 2006

Wasserman, Noah. *The Founder's Dilemmas: Anticipating and Avoiding the Pitfalls That Can Sink a Startup.* Princeton: Princeton University Press, 2012.

Fundraising Planning Models

In *The War For Fundraising Talent*, I have asserted that in many ways the future of the fundraising profession will reveal an increasing divide between those professionals who can effectively accomplish their goals and those who cannot. I believe this divide will be most evident in the professional's ability to understand herself and the organizational culture in which she operates. Even before an initial interview, employers and employees alike will become increasingly savvy in forecasting a successful relationship.

The following four models were designed to allow fundraising professionals and their employers an opportunity to visualize how highly-effective fundraising really works. Each model is designed to ensure that three objectives are consistently achieved.

- First and foremost, we want to ensure that everyone shares a common understanding of highly-effective fundraising practice in advance of any permanent hiring decisions. This means aligning the board, volunteers, management team, staff and volunteers with an understanding of their roles and responsibilities in fundraising, where and how they can make the greatest contributions, and where they can complement the strengths of others.

- Increasing fundraising capacity requires that organizational leaders be able to discern between trivial, meaningful and significant levels of giving. The organization's fundraising philosophy must be informed by a commitment to fewer donors, more meaningful engagement, and direct solicitation. These three deliberate practices are the foundation of a highly effective and successful fundraising program.

- Finally, we want to ensure the organization's ability to identify, train, and retain high-capacity fundraising talent. This begins with understanding the type of individual that will best serve in this role; clearly articulating their goals and objectives; and providing consistent, constructive feedback.

It is human nature for all of us to blame someone or something other than ourselves when something isn't working as well as we'd like. When it comes to fundraising woes in the nonprofit sector, it's especially easy to point fingers at donor attrition, professional turnover, a disengaged board, or a weak economy as the culprits. However, the most entrenched challenges cannot be effectively addressed by casting blame but instead require an understanding of the system that perpetuates our problems. The sector's fundraising challenges are systemic and can only be remedied by restructuring the system.

The *Two Fundraising Cultures* model is a systems archetype which mirrors similar behavioral patterns that are observable in many other aspects of our personal and professional lives. For our purposes, the "shifting the burden archetype" distinguishes between a fundraising culture that consistently shifts the burden for additional support to initial and often trivial gifts versus a culture that relies on meaningful relationships as the pathway to meaningful and significant levels of support. The fundamental solution in the bottom loop is never as immediately attractive as the symptomatic solution that we turn to in the top loop. In order for the fundamental solution to take hold, we often have to redefine the problem itself which often prevents us from assuming the symptomatic solution is the right path to follow.

All nonprofit organizations, large and small, raise funds in accordance with the same basic principles. The extent to which organizations execute their plans efficiently (cost per dollar raised) and effectively (goal achievement) ultimately distinguishes between those organizations that consistently achieve their goals and those that do not. To understand the basic principles, we have designed a systems map that characterizes three lanes, like the three beltway lanes encircling a city, running parallel to each other in concentric circles.

In *The Three Lanes Approach*, each lanes represents an important phase of the fundraising experience that donors inevitably move through as they support an organization's mission. The three lanes approach is not a rigid prescriptive plan; rather it is a below-the-surface understanding of how effective fundraising really works. In addition to providing a framework for planning and evaluating the program's overall performance, the three-lanes approach addresses common roadblocks that organizations routinely encounter as they cultivate their donors through greater levels of commitment as well as the dividing of roles and responsibilities between paid professionals and volunteers, the setting and assessment of goals, and the alignment of the mission.

Each lane is intended to compliment the subsequent lane. The first lane assumes a new donor who may or may not be giving at a level consistent with their capacity. The middle lane assumes an active donor who has expressed a genuine interest in and commitment to the mission through their initial gifts and is receptive to meaningful engagement with the organization. The third lane assumes an active donor who has developed a meaningful relationship with the organization and has made the decision to make a very significant, multi-year commitment to the organization.

The risk inherent in expanding a fundraising program is the application of first lane logic to the subsequent lanes. Lanes two and three are focused on soliciting current donors for subsequent gifts (renewal and stewardship), whereas the first lane is focused on the acquisition of new donors and new gifts. The renewal lanes align closely with indicators of quality relationships and effective goal achievement whereas the first lane aligns with increasing the quantity of relationships and the efficiency with which monies are raised. Whereas the new donor expects to be courted like a new acquaintance, the existing donor prefers being recognized as loyal friend.

Capital campaigns should not be approached as isolated events; rather, they should be integrated into a comprehensive fundraising strategy that begins with the initial gift. Our three-lanes approach coordinates the efforts of a volunteer-driven new acquisition lane with a professionally-driven major gifts program, all intended to work towards the long-term success of a capital growth strategy in lane three. Our approach enables an organization to observe the entire process that begins with an initial gift and eventually arrives at a significant multi-year commitment. The third lane ensures that the organization maintains the greatest flexibility necessary for carefully and strategically responding to the most significant major gift opportunities.

The Effective Campaign Planning model demonstrates the tension inherent in the campaign success curve, the reality of the twelve-year spread, and when to "go to press" with the case for support. It has been my observation that the traditional two-phased approach to campaign planning results in an over-emphasis on the two book-end categories of donors – those giving very large gifts and those giving comparatively smaller ones. This tendency often neglects to make the necessary investment in developing the two middle categories of donors which is also where we tend to see the campaign later lag in performance. This lag in the middle categories can easily account for a 20-30% shortfall in achieving your goal. We have also observed that the two-phased process is overly-reliant on paid professionals in the first half and, in contrast, overly reliant on volunteers in the second half. Our goal is to balance the contributions of professional staff with volunteers throughout the entire campaign.

The **Key Performance Indicators** was discussed at length in the last chapter. This model demonstrates how to prioritize our time with the organization's most valuable donors, how to track and monitor key patterns of work, and how deliberate practices can maximize fundraising performance. This tool is designed to align expectations between the development office, the executive suite and the boardroom.

To learn more about using these fundraising planning models, visit www.lewisfundraising.com/toolbox

To inquire about speaking and consulting engagements, please email me at jason@lewisfundraising.com

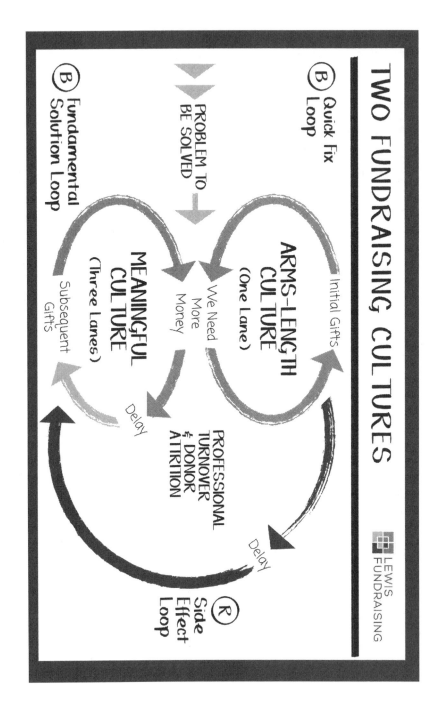

TWO FUNDRAISING CULTURES

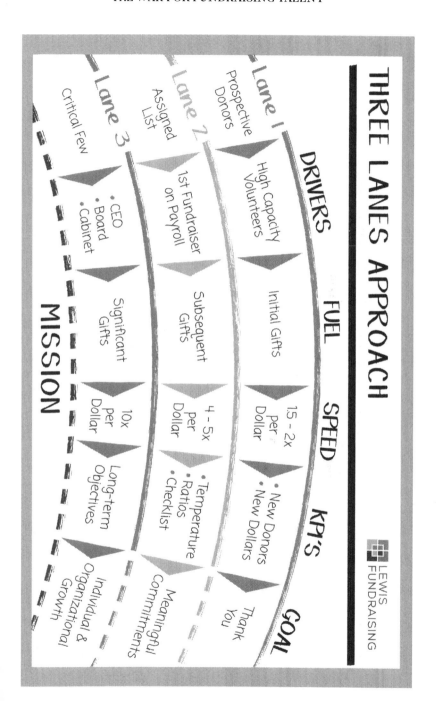

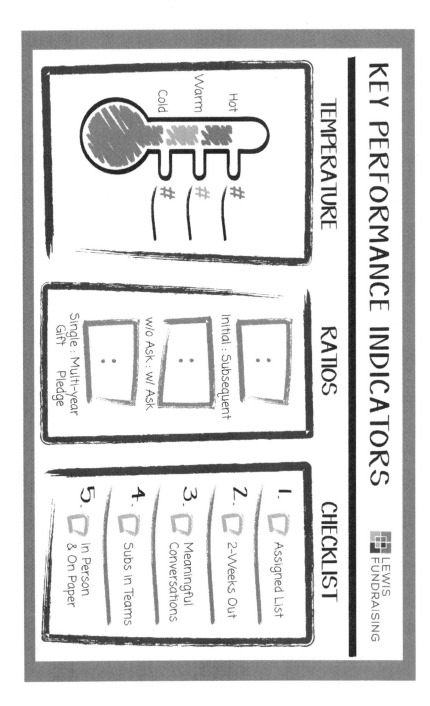

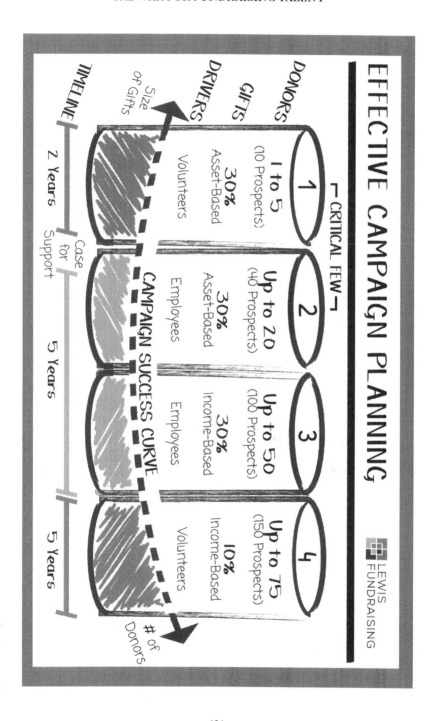

EFFECTIVE CAMPAIGN PLANNING

LEWIS FUNDRAISING

CRITICAL FEW

	1	2	3	4
DONORS	1 to 5 (10 Prospects)	Up to 20 (40 Prospects)	Up to 50 (100 Prospects)	Up to 75 (150 Prospects)
GIFTS	30% Asset-Based	30% Asset-Based	30% Income-Based	10% Income-Based
DRIVERS	Volunteers	Employees	Employees	Volunteers

Size of Gifts

CAMPAIGN SUCCESS CURVE

# of Donors

TIMELINE	2 Years	5 Years	5 Years
	Case for Support		

91057727R00079

Made in the USA
Lexington, KY
18 June 2018